Principled Power

Principled Power

Restoring Democracy and
Opportunity to Polarized America

S. J. REYNOLDS

For information about permissions to reproduce selections from this book, or
for information about special discounts for bulk purchases, please contact info@
principled-power.org

ISBN-10: 0998893110
ISBN-13: 978-0-9988931-1-2
Library of Congress Control Number: 2019904131

Jefferson Hamilton LLC
301 N. Harrison Street, Suite 9F, Princeton, NJ 08540
www.jefferson-hamilton.com

1 2 3 4 5 6 7 8 9 0

For Abby

Contents

Introduction

This book is for those Americans who feel our nation is becoming less and less a land of opportunity and of freedom, and who feel that the state of our politics is a key part of the problem.

Those Americans include many in the working and middle classes for whom this lack of opportunity, and a loss of future prospects, is still relatively new. Those Americans also include minorities and the poor, for whom lack of opportunity is nothing new at all. And they even include many who have known opportunity all their lives yet see a future of wider uncertainties—parents planning for college expenses, managers battling low-cost foreign competition, and government officials struggling to contain foreign upheaval. This book is for all these people, because they are all connected. More importantly, this book is for those who want to address the problem at its roots.

I am not a politician, a professional writer, or a political science professor. I am a business manager, a National Guard officer, and a suburban dad. I have degrees in American history and business. I started my career as an Army officer, then moved to civilian life. For 15 years I was a manager in medical manufacturing companies before switching to college administration. As a Guardsman, I graduated from the Army's Command & General Staff College. I served tours in Bosnia and Iraq.

Most of my weekends and evenings are occupied with sports for my kids, and with other family chores and events. My wife and I do our best to pay our mortgage and expenses. We try to plan for retirement, aging parents, college tuition, and family healthcare, while being responsible members of our community. I never had a deep interest in politics, as long as the system seemed to be working. Over the last decade however, I perceived things had changed.

To me, as to many others, a fundamental and ominous trend developed in the country's affairs, at the heart of our future and our fortunes. We've had serious domestic and foreign challenges, as all generations do, that required debate and action in both society and government. But over the last decade:

- Our political parties became more polarized, fueled by mutual mistrust and acrimony.
- National action of any type became trapped by deadlocked politics, as each party obstructed almost any measure by the other.
- We had multiple government shutdowns over policy disagreements, and a downgraded national credit rating.
- We had the least productive Congresses in a generation.
- A majority of Americans came to believe the country was on the wrong track.

As our dysfunction deepened, I felt compelled to write this book, using what little free time I have between other responsibilities. I've written on nights, weekends, in the parked car during kids' sports practices, and anywhere else I could find some time during the last three years. I felt that American politics had ceased functioning effectively, threatening America's prosperity and leadership, and I wanted to do whatever I could to correct it.

Then in 2016, we had an election that in part was a referendum on whether "the system"—the government specifically and the political and economic establishment more generally—was serving the needs of the nation and especially the middle and working classes. Donald Trump narrowly won the presidency running as an outsider who would serve those needs. But despite his victory, the underlying political system and our polarization remain, and with them the long-term likelihood of continued dysfunction in government and limited opportunity in the economy for most people.

America is supposed to be where political freedom and economic opportunity work together to provide justice and prosperity. Yet for most of us, neither politics nor economics are functioning well separately, much less together. In response, this book presents a clear path for restoring real and enduring function to our politics and government so we can restore opportunity for everyone, not just those at the top. And we can do this by understanding our dysfunctions and their solutions through the twin realities of our national principles, and of national power.

National principles are embodied in the Declaration of Independence and the Constitution, and in our broadly-shared ideals of freedom, opportunity, and justice. National power is a well-studied but little-discussed measure of national capacity and will. And while these are topics of serious study and research for some, this is not a book of scholarship, but of advocacy, and of applied principle. Based on my experience in business, the military, and higher education, this book advocates for an updated theory of national power that, applied in accordance with our national principles, can restore what we are losing: our opportunity, our democracy, and the prosperity and justice they allow.

To do this, the book follows a straightforward path in five chapters.

1. The first chapter, *Where We Are*, opens by describing how our national aspirations of economic opportunity and democratic freedom are overshadowed by the income stagnation and political dysfunction we see continuing every year. Periodically, I include personal experiences to illustrate key points. The chapter then focuses on political dysfunction specifically, showing how it is driven largely by distorted election laws and the media environment. These have combined to create intense polarization and deadlock, preventing coordinated solutions to economic and other problems and seriously raising the specter of national decline.

2. *Principles*. This chapter is the heart of the book. It starts with our national principles as put forth in the Constitution and relates them to the principles of national power. From these come the book's central concept: Principled Power, advocating for a new politics focused on rebuilding and sustaining national power

through efficient, adaptable government and broad economic access. Anchored by the Constitution, Principled Power provides a foundation for reforms to electoral laws and government policy making, each described in a following chapter, that can regain our aspirations by refocusing on our principles.

3. *Power Politics* describes reforms for adaptable government, based on political incentives for leaders to decide and conclude national issues without deadlock. The first half describes how we've skewed these incentives in recent decades through distorted electoral financing and distorted voting practices. The second half describes how Principled Power can motivate partisan-neutral reform to realign the incentives. These reforms include Constitutional authority for Congress to control paid anonymous speech, and an Electoral Reform Act against practices that amplify political extremism.

4. *Power Policy* describes reforms for policy making, based on our first principles of government and its role in maintaining national power. In the early twenty first century, we have costly and mistrusted government, unequal economic opportunity, and deadlocked policy making. The chapter shows how Principled Power can address these critical challenges and others through the broader use of national commissions for policy making, with a focus on overhauling government efficiency, and expanding economic access especially for the working class.

5. *Choosing Our Future.* The final chapter offers alternative visions of American society and politics at midcentury.

One is based on continuing as we are, with our divided politics and economy, while another is based on political and government reform as described in the book. In a third alternative, unaddressed grievances tip our political system to crisis, with major upheaval. The choice among these is ours.

The conclusion is a final call to action, highlighting the tangible, straightforward actions that we can and must take as individual citizens to realign our politics and our economy in accordance with our national principles.

The principles captured in the Declaration and the Constitution are a link to history and to human fundamentals, and have provided an anchor for the United States in the gales of each new age. And these principles are also a polestar for the future—a reference by which we chart a true course. With the world's increasing complexity and information overload, never has a guide been more needed. This book knows that we are indeed losing our way, and shows how we can find it again.

One

Aspirations

*A*s Americans, we aspire to be a model republic—a pluralistic society under the rule of law, where all citizens have
the opportunity to prosper according to their talents.

This book advocates for applying our national principles to
reform political and government dysfunction. But what are our national principles—as Americans, what do we believe in? As a country of 300 million and growing, this might be a question with 300
million different answers. But in general, from our shared history
and culture, there are a relatively few key ideals to which we clas-
sically ascribe our American exceptionalism. These ideals include:

- Government by, for, and of the people
- Self-evident truths

- o All are created equal
- o We are endowed with inalienable rights, including life, liberty, and the pursuit of happiness
- Separation of powers, with checks and balances
- The Rule of Law
  - o Created by elected representatives
  - o Administered by a President and appointed deputies
  - o Interpreted by the judiciary
- Freedom of speech, worship, and association
- Democracy over tyranny
- The melting pot
- Opportunity
- Ingenuity
- Self-reliance
- Can-do optimism
- Property rights
- Free enterprise
- Protection of the minority
- Justice for all

In short, we believe in the principles of political freedom written in both the Declaration of Independence and the Constitution, and we believe in the economic opportunity they create. This is not a complete list, any reader can certainly add more. These are the good things: what we're proud of in the past and aspire to continue in the future.

Is this list a true picture? Not always. Like all nations, we lurch between crises and issues, real and inflated, making our way among, and as part of, the historical forces of our time. As these pages acknowledge, we have major challenges and threats, many of our own making. We are human, and imperfect.

But our shared ideals, whether or not fully attainable, are a critical point of orientation. They remind us of what we want to be as a nation—and even what the world needs us to be.

But recently, we see less and less of the ideal, and less of our potential to reach it.

Americans have increasingly sensed this for the last two decades. Satisfaction with how things are going in the US declined every year in a poll from a high in 2000 to an all-time low in 2008, and remained stubbornly low ever since. Polls of public trust in the US government also declined to and remain at all-time lows in the same period. By 2014, other polls showed large majorities of Americans felt the country's best years were behind them, and that the next generation would be worse off than theirs.[1] This measure is historically significant, higher than any time since the 1950s—beyond Sputnik, Vietnam, the 1973 oil embargo, the Soviet invasion of Afghanistan, and the deficits of the 1980s.[2] In 2016, enough voters agreed with Donald Trump on the need to "make America great again" to elect him President despite his having never served in government or the military.

We might even wonder whether American democracy is past its prime. Is it possible that different political systems are better suited to the 21st century—perhaps China's one-party rule, or Scandinavia's social democracy? Neither is better suited to America than its own Constitutional system, when it is functioning as intended—to fulfill the just roles of government. But the system is clearly not functioning as intended.

Simply put, our current political dysfunction threatens to

divert us so far from our ideals that other systems of government may prove more effective than America's, by our own default.

Challenges
In the face of both domestic and international challenges, it is primarily political dysfunction that threatens us with the real prospect of national decline.

We in the United States have serious challenges both domestically and internationally with an economy and government that are each only partly functioning. Despite this, we've taken decreasing national action every year for a decade. Under both the Obama and Trump administrations, Congress's average output of substantive laws has been 30% lower than under any other administration following World War II.[3]

<u>Domestic Challenges</u>. Domestically, our most critical challenges cover a wide range, including the level of taxes and government spending, economic freedom versus economic inequality, energy needs versus environmental needs, healthcare structure, education, national R&D investment, and infrastructure maintenance. In the face of these challenges, we have strong economic resources, with record corporate profits and the highest average income of the major nations.

And yet, we also have persistent "underemployment" and the highest income inequality of the major nations. We lag behind the rest of the developed world in infant mortality, elementary school enrollment, and life expectancy, and we have the highest rates of incarceration. We are a rich nation which has a vast population struggling, and often failing, to make ends meet.

And in debating what we are as a nation, this is among the most critical realities we face. Despite our vast national resources, working class people are trapped, facing serious economic challenges with little mobility. At the very bottom people face low-paying jobs, indecent housing, no access to effective schools, and poor nutrition. The adults can't improve their station or get out, because there is no path to do it. The kids can't improve their station or get out, because there are few people to show them how.

In our increasingly complex and technical economy, hard work and force of will are rarely enough to achieve prosperity. The well-off have the time and resources to invest in education and pursue opportunity, while most other people must work extremely hard just to survive. They have no additional time to invest in improving their own situation, or their children's situation. Whether we believe that this is an injustice or is just the natural order of modern economic life, it is fair to say that at the very bottom, 45 million people living under the poverty line, spending most of their time trying to survive on minimum wage or less, is a vast waste of human potential.

And this struggle does not stop at the poverty line. Increasingly, the urban middle class that was built in the 20th century on skilled manufacturing jobs was left increasingly in the early 21st century with only unskilled jobs in the service sector; and even then, with not enough of them. In the decade following the financial crisis of 2008 the unemployment rate slowly recovered from its high of 10%; yet even below 5%, for every person unemployed there was another whose employment was only part-time, despite needing full-time work. And most telling of all, the average wage has barely changed at all—not only since 2008, but since 1968.[4]

In the meantime, corporations have grown by small productivity increases and by spreading overseas (often simultaneously), moving not only manufacturing jobs to other countries or to automated systems, but professional jobs as well. While resulting higher corporate profits benefit those with savings to invest in stocks, profits rarely help the middle classes and below who, without good jobs producing income to save and invest in the stock market, are left further and further behind.

Additionally, racial tensions have grown. News stories and videos of unarmed black men shot by police spark protests about not only police use of force, but also a broader suppression of minorities' voting rights and civil liberties. Counter movements on behalf of law enforcement gain support when minority protests intensify to riots like in Ferguson, Missouri, or when police are shot in retaliation for minority deaths. In 2016, Donald Trump's electoral success was largely attributed to white voters energized by visions of returning to times of past national greatness. Yet minorities remember those as times of oppression and struggle, and are unnerved at such white enthusiasm. Even when shootings, protests and debates subside, the tension remains, with no end in sight.

And so, despite periodic bull stock markets and corporate successes, it is clear that the nation will continue to struggle, politically, economically, and socially, until there is broader access to economic opportunity at all levels of society. The challenge is daunting, but millions of American citizens need the nation to do better.

International Challenges. On the international stage, our challenges are no less significant, including globalization, Chinese economic influence, Russian ambitions, nuclear proliferation, climate change, terrorism, and Mideast instability. In 2014, international affairs author Thomas Friedman described this environment as being marked by its general increase in *disorder*, amid which American leadership and concerted western action in general—the "forces of order"—are less in control, with increasingly chaotic consequences.[5]

———

D oes American leadership matter? In a heavy snowstorm in January, 1996, I crossed an Army pontoon bridge over the Sava River from Croatia to Bosnia. I was a lieutenant in the 1st Armored Division, which had moved its 20,000 soldiers, 300 Abrams tanks and 200 Bradley fighting vehicles overland from Germany to implement the Dayton Peace Accords. The Accords ended the 5-year civil war in the former Yugoslavia, where violence erupted in the power vacuum following the fall of the Berlin Wall and the death of the Soviet-backed dictator who had ruled since WWII.

The civil war raged on Europe's doorstep while the western powers struggled to find the shared political will to intervene without being inextricably mired as well. After over 100,000 deaths, and atrocities including the multi-year televised siege of the city of Sarajevo, a US-led NATO bombing campaign against Serbia forced its final agreement to peace terms ending the fighting. A combined NATO land force arrived to occupy an agreed Zone of Separation between the combatants.

After crossing the river, we drove for two straight days over narrow, icy mountain roads to the mining town of Olovo, where the unit would spend the next nine months, monitoring the peace and returning some stability to the area. The Zone of Separation, ZOS, had generally been drawn along the front lines on the date of the peace agreement, and there was no doubt that Olovo had been on the front lines for some time. It was set in a narrow mountain valley with a river and the main road running down the center, with the Serbs on one side, and the Bosnians on the other. The town was a burned-out, pock-marked, snow-covered wasteland that resembled pictures of thousands of similarly-destroyed towns from World War II.

Our unit focused most of its efforts on operating checkpoints, meeting with locals to ensure there were no active military units or militia in the area, escorting logistics and humanitarian convoys, and improving our austere living conditions. As soldiers, we didn't enjoy it much, because it was more tedious than we had expected. But we had trained a long time for it, and it was gratifying to see it come together successfully.

Despite the burning hatred felt between the Bosnians and Serbs after inflicting terrible atrocities on each other over several years, most of the people wanted the Americans there to end the fighting. By being there, we were providing stability not just to Bosnia and the former Yugoslavia, but as an active example of continued American leadership in a world wondering what the new world order would look like after the Cold War. We were where we needed to be at the time.

———

In his book *Every Nation for Itself*,[6] author Ian Bremmer assesses that the relative decline of the US against other ambitious powers is evolving from the dominance of the industrial G7 (or G8, or

G20) to become the multipolar *G-Zero World*. In this new environment, he sees that no single country or alliance is meeting the challenge of global leadership that has emerged in the power vacuum following the Cold War, because none has sufficient power to unilaterally impose solutions to our shared challenges.

In this increasingly prevalent world, Bremmer predicts the relative losers will be the major-power absolutists vying to achieve or maintain dominance, along with those who are either dependent or parasites on larger neighbors, such as Mexico or Ukraine. The winners will be so-called pivot states, such as Turkey or Brazil, which accept the new world as it is, and play the middle ground. Other groups who play the middle ground will also benefit, such as financial firms that move operations to unregulated countries.

It is a sobering picture of an international free-for-all where, at best, the world will struggle to find coordinated solutions to global problems, and at worst, might see dramatic increases of war, economic instability, and deprivation.

Decline?

In the face of these challenges both international and domestic, there *should* be some hope in that America, as the world's leading military and economic power, has a system of government that is designed to adapt to problems and is capable of providing beneficial order. However, several distortions of our original system have increasingly paralyzed our nation's ability to adapt, with ominous consequences.

Within the US over the last decade, top scholars and analysts have been engaged in an important debate about whether the US, or even the West more broadly, is in decline—either relative to other nations such as China and India, or absolutely. Disturbingly, few such observers have attempted to suggest specific and feasible measures in response. The key conclusions of five of the most important experts are described below, including their analysis of the underlying problems and their potential solutions.

<u>Dysfunctional Politics</u>. First in 2008, Foreign Affairs editor and CNN commentator Fareed Zakaria published *The Post-American World*. In it, he argues that by our very success in exemplifying and spreading liberal democracy, the US has increased effective competition against itself, and it is essential that we adapt to this evolving world to maintain our leadership.[7]

He writes that, in our favor, we are still by far the most innovative and productive nation—a highly dynamic economy at the cutting edge, and the most competitive major economy in the world. Yet, in spite of this, the nation's chief limitation is the state of persistent deadlock in Washington. He says that America

"has developed a highly dysfunctional politics. An antiquated and overly rigid political system to begin with—about 225 years old—has been captured by money, special interests, a sensationalist media, and ideological attack groups. ... A 'can-do' country is now saddled with a 'do-nothing' political process, designed for partisan battle rather than problem solving."[8]

And without problem-solving at the national level, we cannot continue to compete. "The real test for the United States is political," he says, "and it rests not just with America at large but with Washington in particular. Can Washington adjust and adapt to a world in which others have moved up? Can it respond to shifts in economic and political power?"[9] In summary, at the same time our own successes have inspired increasing economic and military competition, we are weakening ourselves by domestic political dysfunction.

In 2011, British historian and Harvard professor Niall Ferguson expanded on these trends, offering a starker assessment of the US trajectory (and that of the West in general) in *Civilization: The West and the Rest*. Ferguson agrees with Zakaria that the US and other western nations face increasing challenges, citing economic decline against China, financial fragility, and a new lack of confidence in the model of western society.[10]

Also like Zakaria, Ferguson says that despite these, the west still retains the advantage of innovation. Innovation is not easily imitated, because it must exist alongside functional political institutions: "Western civilization is more than just one thing; it is a package. It is about political pluralism ... as well as capitalism; it is about freedom of thought as well as scientific method; it is about the rule of law and property rights as well as democracy."

Despite these advantages, Ferguson says, western success is very much in doubt, hanging on "whether we are still able to recognize the superiority of that package."[11] For Ferguson, our greatest peril may be chronically failing to appreciate the importance of these institutions to western success, or to teach this to new generations. Further, Ferguson shows that through history, when leading systems decline, it often isn't slow or gentle. It can be sudden and dramatic, like the collapse of the Soviet Union in 1991, or the collapse of Wall Street in 2008—the stakes of dominance and decline are serious indeed.

So, while Zakaria is specific about what most endangers the US (political dysfunction), and Ferguson is more general, the implication is the same: the success of the nation rests on the health of our political institutions, and we neglect them at our peril.

In 2014, Stanford professor Francis Fukuyama published *Political Order and Political Decay.*[12] In 1989, Fukuyama had written the essay "*The End of History?*" in which he argued that "liberal democracy stood alone as the only form of government compatible with socio-economic modernity".[13] This later book provides a detailed nonpartisan history and analysis of democratic political institutions, illustrating their common factors of success, and their common potential for decay.

Focusing on America's current situation, Fukuyama is very clear (like Zakaria and Ferguson) that America's greatest strength has always been its innovative private sector. And he further agrees with them that America's greatest challenge is the state of politics. (None says that politics is blocking innovation directly, but rather that politics prevents the full benefits of the innovation economy from being realized nationwide, a theme the next chapters will address more fully.) From Fukuyama's perspective, America's political system is undergoing a decay by which "many specific American political institutions have become dysfunctional,"[14] with high barriers to reform.

Among these barriers, he says, the most daunting is that all political insiders are part of a system they are unwilling or unable to change, by which "political parties have become hostage to powerful interest groups that do not represent the American electorate."[15] This has effectively transformed the US into a "vetocracy", used by special interest groups to hold almost any decision hostage to narrow agendas. And although Fukuyama wrote two years before the election of Donald Trump, who was not a political insider when he ran, Fukuyama might also point out that neither do billionaires, such as Trump, represent the American electorate.

Combined with political polarization, such a vetocracy can move neither forward nor backward, as epitomized by the US political deadlock on taxes and government finance. Such deadlock, he says, has further combined with our historic distrust of government to get us stuck in a "bad equilibrium". In it, "low-quality government breeds distrust on the part of the citizens, who then withhold from the state both the compliance and resources [taxes] necessary for the state to function effectively", confirming the original distrust in a self-fulfilling prophesy.

These authors all wrote before the election campaigns of 2016 and the rise of Donald Trump, and while they differ in manner and approach, their common themes are as striking as they are sobering. They all say that US strength, like Western strength in general, is driven primarily by the vitality of the private sector and its capacity for continued innovation. However, high-functioning democratic political institutions and public confidence are also essential. And in the face of surging economic and geo-political competition, it is the current dysfunction of American political institutions that is our greatest weakness, preventing effective response to national issues and damaging public confidence.

Populist Backlash. The election of 2016 proved the point abruptly, when Donald Trump channeled public distrust against elites of both parties, and against the post-war economic system more generally. His campaign themes were to Make America Great Again, to construct a border wall with Mexico, and to bring back outsourced manufacturing jobs; generally considered a populist- and nationalist-themed platform.

Populism and nationalism advanced in other Western nations as well in 2016-2017. Within six months either side of the 2016 US election, the British narrowly voted to leave the European Union, and populist parties gained significant new voter support and parliament seats in Germany, The Netherlands, and Italy, among others. France notably resisted the trend that year, electing progressive-centrist Emmanuel Macron as President in 2017. Because the populist movements were heavily supported by white native-born voters in each country, they have also been labeled nativist or ethnic-nationalist.

Following these developments, additional authors have addressed the question of decline. in 2017, Edward Luce published *The Retreat of Western Liberalism*. In it, he frames the populist surge around 2016 as a middle- and working-class reaction to their perceived loss of economic security and political power. He describes how, in the previous decades, the West's liberal democratic governments integrated the world economy, and businesses intensified automation. This created jobs and expanded markets in the developing world, reducing poverty there. But in the developed world it only grew incomes for the best-off—the managers and professionals who had a stake in the higher profits from outsourcing. Middle class wages were flat, with high unemployment after the financial crash of 2009.[16]

Luce says that because liberal democratic governments were unresponsive to middle class economic stagnation, populists and nationalists such as Trump gained supporters. The populists focused on building pride in traditional culture and past successes, promising a return to a more prosperous time, with more middle class jobs in manufacturing and mining, and less immigration and trade that seem to have taken those jobs. "The world's elites have helped provoke what they feared," Luce writes, "a populist uprising against the world economy. Globalization is going into reverse just as the impact of new technology is showing signs of picking up."[17]

In 2018, Steven Brill published *Tailspin*, arguing that rising economic inequality, and the special interests and vetocracy it engendered, has driven a fifty-year decline in America. Like Luce, he says the elites—professionals, entrepreneurs, and managers—are primarily responsible for the decline, and he focuses the book on describing its origins and possible solutions.[18] The source of it all, he says, is that "The most talented, driven Americans chased the American dream—and won it for themselves. [Then they were able to] outsmart and co-opt the government that might have reined them in, and pull up the ladder so more could not share in their success or challenge their primacy."[19]

As he describes, this started in the 1960s, when the liberal impulse to fairness and equity created America's modern meritocracy by opening up top colleges to high performers regardless of background. The high performers then captured the meritocracy in perpetuity by investing in what amount to moats, to protect their privilege. These moats start with expensive college preparation for children to get the best educations and jobs. Moats also include campaign finance laws that helped corporate lobbyists to weaken middle and working class unions; and include tax laws by which the wealthy minimize their taxes and retain wealth. Brill says that as a result, our most important divide is not actually the one between the political parties, but between those who are protected—from financial uncertainty by wealth and education—and those who are unprotected.

In telling this story, Brill is essentially providing the deep historical details behind the special interests, entrenched actors, and vetocracy outlined by Zakaria and Fukuyama. He is also providing the details behind Fukuyama's bad equilibrium, in which middle-class distrust and poorly-functioning government reinforce each other. While Brill has deeper detail than Luce on the sources of inequality in the US, he doesn't address the populist backlash or its implications, as Luce does.

A final major element of the populist backlash and the question of decline is the role of identity politics, which both Luce and Fukuyama address. For Luce, identity politics were certainly relevant for Donald Trump's political rise and his power base. But Luce sees identity as secondary to the more fundamental element of economic insecurity. After all, he says, "Millions who backed Trump in 2016 had voted for Barack Obama back in 2008. Did they suddenly become deplorable? A better explanation is that many kinds of Americans have long felt alienated from an establishment that has sidelined their economic complaints."[20]

However, Luce still acknowledges that the perception of being displaced economically and politically by newcomers created resentment among many whites, which Trump and other populists used as a tool to gain support. "Obama offered hope... Trump channeled rage... by giving a higher priority to the politics of ethnic identity than people's common interests, the American left helped to create what it feared." He then quotes professor and self-described liberal Mark Lilla: "'Those who play the identity game should be prepared to lose it.'"[21]

In 2018, Fukuyama published *Identity*, in which he steps back from the 2016 election to put the rise of ethnic nationalism in wider historical context.[22] His thesis is that the sense of one's identity group, and especially its level of respect in society, has long driven human affairs. In recent decades in the US, he says, both the left and the right re-defined their focus from economic issues to identity issues—advocating for rights and respect for various identity groups. The upside of the trend is that the privileged can become more aware of how they affect the un-privileged. For the downside he agrees with Luce: identity politics "have become a cheap substitute for serious thinking about how to reverse the thirty-year trend in most liberal democracies toward greater socio-economic inequalities."[23]

This is how the debate on decline has evolved since 2016. Before that election, it was already becoming clear that our greatest strength (industrial and technology innovation) was being undermined by an expanding cycle of political dysfunction and of the public mistrust of politics and government that resulted. Then the rise of populist nationalism and Trump's election channeled that mistrust into political power.

The most important driver of mistrust was economic decline for the middle and working class—though this was largely overshadowed by an increasing political focus on promoting identity groups, including political party identity. Yet the longer-standing problem of vetocracy by special interests remains. Elites—those Brill calls the protected—use vetocracy with increased intensity to defend economic interests and the status quo, and each party uses it to obstruct the other. And so the situation persists as it did before 2016; political dysfunction remains our greatest weakness.

<u>What Can We Do?</u> Unfortunately, these writers only offer generalities. Zakaria provides six concepts for how leaders might adapt policy in the new world. They are clearly aimed at the President, cabinet, and other top-level leaders, and focus on how the US should most productively engage internationally. But they do not address the chief weakness of political dysfunction.

Ferguson likewise avoids specific solutions. He says that we need to better understand the history and success factors of western civilization as he's described them, so we can build on them to meet our challenges effectively. This requires better scholarship and education for future leaders, and an informed citizenry.

Fukuyama's *Political Order and Political Decay*, while entirely focused on understanding political decay, is also limited only to general concepts regarding solutions. (That said, his prescriptions align with the more specific proposals outlined later in this book.) He has three main points, addressing decay by vetocracy and the "entrenched actors" perpetuating it.

First, Fukuyama recommends "mechanisms to promote stronger hierarchical authority within the existing system of separated powers"—mechanisms that allow for more rational planning and decision-making while not limiting democratic participation. Second is to "trim veto points", that is, reduce the places in the political process where special interest groups can hold progress hostage to narrow demands.

Finally, Fukuyama says, "a reform coalition has to emerge that unites groups that don't have a stake in the current system." But this is easier said than done, he warns, since "they need leadership and a clear-cut agenda, which is not automatically forthcoming."[24] (Published two years before the presidential election of 2016, this was prescient of Donald Trump and Bernie Sanders, who both ran as outsiders. But while Sanders talked more frequently about reforming the political system itself, Trump focused the majority of his campaign on other issues such as curtailing trade deals and immigration. So while Trump did indeed provide both leadership and a clear-cut agenda for some outsider groups as Fukuyama suggested, an agenda to counteract political decay was not forthcoming.)

Luce's solutions are more brief. He states his book's aim is not to provide a policy manifesto, so like Zakaria, he provides only a short list of high-level goals for western governments. They are focused on domestic policies that would address the stagnant middle class's underlying grievances, on a progressive model: government supplied health care, worker retraining, and secure borders that are humanely enforced.

Further, he urges the ruling elites to lead these changes themselves, because "There is no rule that says populists fizzle out." While he predicts the Trump policies will not succeed in improving middle class lives, in an echo of Ferguson's warnings of collapse Luce says, "There will be a lethal mood of betrayal and frustration when he fails. ... As president, the means at Trump's disposal to divert public anger and target his enemies are chilling."[25] However, beyond his high-level policy recommendations, Luce does not discuss pathways for elites to lead change—that is, activities or messages to counter populism and move towards the policies he suggests.

Steven Brill dedicates much more space to solutions, outlining the work of visionaries and reformers who are addressing the factors of our tailspin—meritocracy of the wealthy, money in politics, middle class job loss. Each of the solutions he describes is specific, several of them have been proven at small scale, and they only need public and political support to be instituted more broadly.

But Brill is vague about what might motivate support for each solution, and is also vague about how to tie the reforms together. He suggests that outrage and disgust over inequities will lead to broad support for wise solutions—a storming of the moats.[26] While this sounds a hopeful note, it opens the question of how outrage and disgust are likely to be channeled so productively. As Luce says, populist leaders can channel public anger *against* the experts and their wise solutions as easily as for them.

Finally, Fukuyama outlines solutions to the problem of identity politics. As the driver of human affairs, he says, identity can be the remedy for populist politics if it is used to integrate instead of to divide. To do this, he says nations should deliberately promote national identities of creed, based on sources of unity: constitutionalism, rule of law, and human equality.

For example, the US could revitalize civics education in public schools, and require national service for all youth, whether military service or otherwise. And he says we should comprehensively reform immigration policy to alleviate its effect as a persistent source of racial and economic resentment. But he acknowledges that political will is lacking for all of these, blocked by the vetocracy he identified in his earlier book. Comprehensive solutions are unlikely in the face of political deadlock.[27]

These authors, each from different perspectives and over the period of a decade, agree that the dysfunction of our political

institutions is our greatest weakness. Our main strength, innovation, has resumed providing economic growth after years of
recession. But the growth is still captured by the well-off, who
have used their resources to enact laws and train their children to
maintain access to wealth and to political power.

Meanwhile, economic stress for the middle class and below,
amid rising focus on identity politics and immigration, has made
many whites in the middle and working class open to leaders
who channel discontent at government and elites, and who assert
working class rights and identity heritage. But the dysfunction of
vetocracy remains, defined by partisanship and deadlock, which
prevent effective response to national issues and damage public
confidence in a bad equilibrium.

Partisanship and deadlock are the keys. Certainly, we also had
division and discord going back to the nation's founding. From
the time of the Revolution through the nineteenth century, our
politics was even more partisan and vicious than today. We fought
a civil war. But for fifty years after World War II, the president
and Congress proved generally capable of compromise. Even
when government was divided between the parties, our system of
elected representation allowed us to not only adapt to, but to lead
changes in society, politics and economics.[28]

Now however, after a century of leadership in world affairs,
this system is breaking down. A set of minor, seemingly unrelated
features of our electoral system combine with the growth of partisan media to reward the extremism and deadlock we see in politics
today. But as the rest of this chapter will argue, these electoral
features are distortions, and are serving to undermine the most
fundamental principles on which American government is based.

And so it is towards the distortions that we need to focus our most urgent efforts. We can and must restore our national governance and our national power, for the sake of ourselves, our neighbors, and our children, and as an example to others around the world.

———

I was driving with my 9- and 10-year-old when a news story on the radio made a passing reference to the Cold War, and both of the kids asked what "Cold War" meant. Until then, I hadn't given much thought to the fact that the end of the Cold War is a very tangible way that the next generation's world is fundamentally different from those before it.

The Berlin Wall came down in 1989, but I clearly remember that only five years before, the TV movie *The Day After* presented a vision of a nuclear attack on an American city, making such an impression that the next day several of my high school classes put aside the planned lessons for the day to discuss it. Our kids today are lucky not to be growing up with the fear of annihilation like we had before the 90's, but it raises the question of our national purpose.

From WWII to 1990, America was the Leader of the Free World, locked in existential struggle with totalitarianism. Ten years later, we had 9/11 and the financial crisis. In living memory, we've almost always had an existential national threat. Now, we've finally got some breathing space—what will we do with it? Where are we going?

We need to think and talk openly about our national purpose. Is our nation just an economic free-for-all until the next crisis gives us somewhere else to focus attention? The question of the role of government is not merely a matter of balancing taxes and intrusiveness against the need for social services, but of what the nation means, and why our government was established in the first place. If we understand the answers to these questions, the answer to the size and role of government will follow.

Political Deadlock and Its Drivers

Our biggest national challenge is that in the face of our problems, our political system is mired in deadlock. In the mid-1990s Republicans in Congress under the leadership of Newt Gingrich tested a strategy of government shutdowns to block Bill Clinton's agenda. Then Democrats blocked George W. Bush's agenda where they could after 2000, and the Republicans subsequently blocked Barack Obama even more intensely than they blocked Clinton. The trend shows little sign of ending with Democrats in opposition to Donald Trump, with the promise of continued deadlock as a result.

What is fundamentally driving this deadlock? Is there a way to address it at its source? While the answers are complex, we can start with the simple observation that we have a generally even balance of power between the major parties in Congress, especially in the Senate. If our political environment focused on the public good and rewarded compromise, this balance of power would not necessarily be a bad thing. To the contrary, it could be relatively efficient, since it requires bi-partisan collaboration to pass legislation.

Instead, our electoral distortions and our media environment reward far more destructive behavior. The incentives are for politicians to appeal to their partisan bases in two relatively new ways. The first is adopting a rhetoric of uncompromising party purity, using the media to spread it not only on campaign but also while in government. And second is using any legal means possible to derail the other party.

The result of the first is what professors Amy Gutman and Dennis Thompson, in their book *The Spirit of Compromise*, have memorably named the "permanent campaign".[29] With the most sophisticated modern techniques of advertising and marketing science, the political parties and their candidates use the media to amplify negative emotions and fear about the other party, creating an uncompromising, polarizing acrimony.

The second, using any means possible, is what professors Steven Levitsky and Daniel Ziblatt described in *How Democracies Die* as the abandonment of two longstanding practices or norms essential for well-functioning democracy: mutual toleration of rivals, and forbearance in the exercise of power. Without mutual toleration, politicians do not accept rivals as legitimate or loyal, to be heard or respected whether in or out of power. Without forbearance, leaders more readily exercise legal rights against rivals, even if it harms the democratic function of the overall system. We abandoned both of these norms, they say, with the rhetoric of the permanent campaign, and with our strategies of blocking any progress by the other party.[30]

The combined effect—of the loss of norms and the permanent campaign—is not just political disagreement. The effect is deep suspicion or outright hatred by ever more voters in each party toward the other, so that even the motivations of the other party to support America's best interests are suspect.

Increasingly for the major parties and their leaders, the goal in national politics seems to be less and less about solving major national issues quickly in the interests of constituents or of the country. Now, the goal is to win a filibuster-proof super-majority in Congress, in order to enact an agenda free of debate or compromise with the other party.

Out of this has grown the strategy of obstruction and its attendant pathologies. The obstruction creates dysfunction that can be blamed on the rival party, justifying campaigns to vote out the rival party en masse. In a related practice, extremist factions can hold progress, any progress, hostage to ideological demands, scuttling bills to prevent the opposing party or opposing factions from advancing an agenda and building political momentum with voters—Fukuyama's "vetocracy" at work. Although Fukuyama, like Gutman & Thompson, wrote during the Obama administration, the same dynamics continued under President Trump.

Yet, as destructive as they are, these strategies are more symptoms of our dysfunction than its causes. The real roots of our dysfunction are our electoral distortions, which reward and perpetuate divisiveness in government and in our public debates. At the same time, the rapid growth of media since 1990 forced this divisiveness into our daily lives and pushed us to choose sides, with little room in the middle. To seriously address dysfunction, we must understand the electoral distortions and the media environment in detail.

Electoral Distortions. First are the distortions of the electoral system—how politicians gain office and power—that we've allowed to accumulate in recent decades. These provide electoral advantages for more partisan positions and rhetoric among the major parties and their candidates.

The first distortion is due to long-running and seemingly-innocuous voting practices, such as the timing of Election Day on a weekday, and party-specific primary elections. As described in a later chapter, these practices, none of which are mandated by the Constitution, encourage a higher proportion of partisan and ideologically-committed voters to attend the polls. While this is not directly responsible for our current polarization, it creates a fertile ground to maintain it.

Building on this is the second distortion, gerrymandering: the long-running and well-known practice in which state legislatures draw congressional district lines to provide partisan advantage. The Constitution mandates that states adjust congressional districts every ten years following the census, but does not mandate how to do it. As of 2018, state legislatures controlled the redistricting process in 42 of 50 states, so that if one party controls both houses of a state legislature (and especially if the party also has the governorship), it has complete power to set district lines in that party's favor lasting ten years. When manipulated intentionally in this way, regardless of which party sets the lines, the resulting Congressional districts are safe seats—very reliably either Republican or Democrat. These one-party districts favor more party-pure positions among successful candidates, and send more highly-partisan lawmakers to Washington with every election cycle.[31]

Finally, the most recent and clear-cut of these distortions is that we've allowed wealthy campaign donors and corporate lob-byists an outsized voice in elections and in government, through anonymous and unlimited campaign financing that super PACs and 501.c.4 "social welfare groups" enable. Such unlimited and anonymous financing greatly intensifies polarization and dead-lock in two ways. First, in quality, it encourages more extreme rhetoric and positions among candidates—a combative and ideo-logically-charged environment naturally encourages the largest donations from combative and ideologically committed donors.

And second, in quantity, massively increasing funding is mas-sively increasing political messaging, media, punditry, and adver-tising of all types, making partisan rhetoric increasingly ubiquitous in our daily lives. In 1998, total expenditure for Congressional and Senate campaigns was $2.5 billion; by 2018, it was $5.2 bil-lion. Much of the increase was from outside groups (super PACs and non-profits not officially tied to a candidate or party), whose expenditures grew from $10 million to $1.1 billion.[32] Unlimited financing is the fuel for the permanent campaign.

Media Environment. Up until thirty years ago, these distortions might not have had the polarizing effect we see today. However, in the mid-90s an information revolution brought two waves of technology change to the business of media and information, and these waves helped polarize us based on our partisan preferences, and then intensified that polarization to extremism.

In the first wave, cable TV expanded and fragmented the sup-ply of broadcast news media. This initiated our modern polar-ization by a) offering options to indulge partisan preferences in viewing the news—for example, with conservatives preferring Fox

News and liberals using a variety of traditional media sources—and b) sensationalizing the news, especially the drama of partisan argument and standoffs. 24-hour news-as-dramatic-entertainment enabled the permanent campaign by giving it a stage and making it exciting: people tuned in to the latest partisan drama or outrage, selling ad time for news and social media companies, and selling books and speaking engágements for analysts, observers, and consultants.

In the second wave, the internet and later social media created an information free-for-all of atomized and often anonymous interactions that have intensified our cable-TV polarization to extremism. Because web sites earn ad money by keeping viewers engaged and clicking their pages as long as possible, the internet is a highly-competitive "attention economy",[33] in which publishers track what we view, and feed us more of it. By following our own interests, we've sorted ourselves into communities of the like-minded that focus and intensify the shared values within the group, especially regarding culture and politics. The communities become self-selecting tribes, communicating in so-called echo chambers of similar thought, intensifying our cable-TV-derived polarization to extremism.

Further, this information environment enables and rewards tech-driven manipulation, ranging on a spectrum from open partisan messaging and persuasion on one end, to shadowy disinformation and smear campaigns on the other. On the open persuasion end, manipulation takes the form of automated message refinement. In it, algorithms test and refine a political ad, graphic, or story to determine which form stimulates the maximum desired response from a small sample of a target audience, say, voters with a certain political profile. Once the effect of the message is found to be optimal, the final result is automatically sent to the entire targeted group, to affect their opinions and behaviors—with the entire sequence performed by computer programs.[34]

On the disinformation end of the spectrum, manipulation takes the form of so-called fake news—manufactured stories masquerading as legitimate news reports. These are designed to spread false but damaging information about a target subject or group, structured in a way to thrill or enrage a target audience enough to be spread faster than the truth can catch up. Other forms of disinformation include social media posts manufactured and spread automatically by so-called bots. These posts are published in high volume, and appear like a groundswell of group opinion on a certain topic, for the purpose of convincing real group members about a certain point of view, or to take a certain action, such as joining a protest rally.[35]

Significantly, even when such efforts are recognized as false manipulation, they contribute further to polarization and extremism by outraging the target and prompting accusations and investigations of potential culprits. As the accusations and enmity rise, social media companies, news companies, and ad consultants benefit financially, with the nonstop debate sustaining high ratings for the news and high traffic on web sites, all with attendant ad revenues. And this raises the most confounding element. While media certainly provide valued services—personal connections through social media, and public information from news media—they also are players in, and benefit financially from, the intensity of our social divides and the permanent campaign.

Driven as it is by a combination of technology and economics, the media environment will continue to evolve rapidly, and will not be easily controlled by government or any other entity—and given the importance of free speech for democracy, we should be wary of such control. But the media environment has fundamentally changed the landscape of politics, massively expanding the outlets for sophisticated political persuasion, and it is important to remain aware of its key roles in our polarization and dysfunction.

Taken together, electoral distortions and the media environment constitute the systemic drivers of our dysfunction. They are the interlocked system of incentives that drive politicians' strategies and voters' choices, combining nationally to create polarization and deadlock. We've backed into this through the permanent campaign on the 24-hour news cycle, in which elected officials are unable to collaborate or compromise—that is, govern—with members of the other party. If they do compromise, it will be recorded and held against them, often by their own party hardliners, in the next election.

This environment rewards hardened negotiating positions instead of compromise, and has resulted in our multi-year paralyzing deadlock. And political deadlock leads to impending decline: we can see that the government is unable to adapt to national and world developments, much less lead them. Unless we address these interlinked distortions, the deadlock and decline will worsen.

Polarization. Greatly complicating the systemic drivers of dysfunction are the psychological drivers, which have crystalized in the effect of partisan polarization. As our political dysfunction leads to fears of decline, it accelerates the urgency for solutions.

And our urgency has found form and voice at both extremes of the political spectrum.

On the right of the spectrum, the urgency has been embodied in the last decade in the Tea Party and then in Donald Trump's election, with the rallying cries to take the country back from government insiders of both parties for their self-serving big government of tax-and-spend. On the left has been the Occupy movement and the Bernie Sanders campaign protesting the rising inequality maintained by business and political elites to protect their power, and later the Resist movement opposing President Trump.

Racial tensions have added to the sense of urgency. Black voters and increasing numbers of Latino voters largely align with the left, with Black Lives Matter and immigration reform carried as issues of basic human justice. The white working class, while under economic pressures as many minorities are, largely aligns with the right. They often bridle at accusations of racism, with many countering Black Lives Matter and protests against police use of force by saying that "all lives matter", and that law abiding members of minority communities should support police, not protesters.

In the center are moderates of both parties, and independent voters. They often see a deadlocked battleground where leaders of all sides harden their positions against the opposition in the permanent campaign, and where scoring political points and ascribing blame for dysfunction is the main activity.

Ironically perhaps, these reactions by voters on all parts of the spectrum have two key elements in common. First, they are largely driven by a need for economic security for the middle and working class. And second, aside from the race tension, they are largely reactions to what often seems from the outside to be a system of political leadership and wealthy campaign donors that is insular and remote, more dedicated to winning partisan victories than to addressing middle and working class insecurity. As a basis for common cause, these reactions provide a spark of hope for improvement.

This system of donor-driven politics and partisanship has come about gradually over time, so that as a nation we have been slow to recognize it as dangerous, like the frog in the slowly-boiling pot. And in recent years many current and former lawmakers report having a similar experience of gradual recognition in the course of their own political careers. Individually, their intentions are almost always noble—to serve the good of their home communities, and the country.

But more than ever, gaining and maintaining elected office requires a major time commitment to fundraising and to party dogma. This not only takes precious time and resources from representing one's home community in deliberations for the good of the nation, but it makes officeholders beholden to major donors. And while some politicians may argue that donor influence is less true than it seems, the mere appearance is damaging enough, casting doubt on the motives and loyalties of lawmakers' positions and votes individually, and on the legitimacy of Congress as an institution.

As polarization has continued, our political energy has been increasingly focused against the other party—our neighbors and fellow citizens—instead of against all of the other challenges we face.

Because of this, political observers say we are increasingly gripped by *partyism*,[36] not dissimilar to racism or sexism. With partyism, we are increasingly using party affiliation as a basis for judging and all too often dismissing others and their views instantly. The more we sense people categorizing Republicans as uniformly and unbendingly conservative, and Democrats as uniformly and unbendingly liberal, the less inclined we are to listen to each other respectfully and try to work together. Instead we either isolate ourselves in like-minded communities (both physically and online), angrily confront each other, or censor ourselves in mixed company so we are not judged and dismissed. Ultimately, we are stifling trust and community as a nation.

And this has become a feedback loop that defines the politics of our time. Systemic distortions including unlimited anonymous donations, gerrymandering, partisan primaries, the permanent campaign, and obstructionism intensify extremism and deadlock. Extremist deadlock raises the specter of decline, further intensifying our urgency and our polarization, and accelerating the cycle. And over time, the effect of this environment is changing our sense of identity until we are partisans first and fellow Americans second.

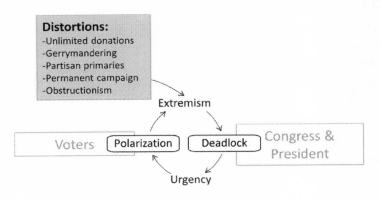

Are we doomed? It hurts to say it, but it is difficult to envision any trajectory but continued deadlock and decline if something doesn't change. Left alone, our current political deadlock will cause us to stagnate, so that we are simply out-maneuvered for leadership in the wider world. We will make fewer and fewer efficient choices, and spiral down.

But we don't have to accept this. If we see this and name it, we can work to overcome it. And we have the means right in front of us. As a nation, we need to return to our first principles.

Two

First Principles

Irst principles are essential to almost every field of human knowledge and endeavor. Formally, a first principle is "a basic, foundational proposition or assumption that cannot be derived from any other."[37] It is an irreducible concept, a fundamental truth. And now, against our increasingly debilitating deadlock, we should turn to our country's first principles for a solution.

We are, after all, a nation of first principles, the self-evident truths

that all men are created equal, that they are endowed by their Creator with certain unalienable Rights, that among these are Life, Liberty and the pursuit of Happiness.— That to secure these rights, Governments are instituted among Men, deriving their just powers from the consent of the governed.[38]

In 1776, we enshrined the principle that government exists to secure citizens' equality and rights to liberty and the pursuit of happiness, and is justified in governing only as far as we, as citizens, say it is. Also:

> —That whenever any Form of Government becomes destructive of these ends, it is the Right of the People to alter or to abolish it, and to institute new Government, laying its foundation on such principles and organizing its powers in such form, as to them shall seem most likely to effect their Safety and Happiness.[39]

So, it is our right to alter our government when it is destructive of liberty and the pursuit of happiness.

In their own time of political turbulence, our founders (most of whom were wary of the firebrands preaching violent revolution) turned to the first principles of the Enlightenment's natural rights of man, and determined that they had to take responsibility for deliberate reform. They disagreed on many fine points, but the principles they did agree on became the Declaration of Independence, to which the founders pledged "our Lives, our Fortunes, and our sacred Honor".[40]

From these principles, and the trial of the American Revolution and resulting peace came the Constitution—a structure to put the principles to action in the face of the need to govern.

The Constitution captures our first principles most fundamentally in its opening sentence, the Preamble. With the Preamble the framers bequeathed us the justification for the singular institution that defines and binds the nation—the United States government. The Preamble says:

We the People ordained and established the Constitution to:

- form a more perfect Union,
- establish Justice,
- ensure domestic Tranquility,
- provide for the common defense,
- promote the general Welfare,
- and secure the Blessings of Liberty to ourselves and our Posterity.[41]

Significantly, the only two substantive words common to these seminal passages of the Declaration and the Constitution are "secure" and "Liberty". By the Declaration, securing rights—liberty—is the just purpose of any government. By the Constitution, it is the final purpose of *our* government. Securing liberty is the preeminent reason the nation exists; it is our national purpose, and a mandate.

The framers' focus on securing liberty is well established by historians, even if it is little known by the general public. The framers knew that democracy first and foremost required security, and security required a strong central government uniting the states. That is why securing liberty is the first and most enduring purpose of the Constitution, and why we are the United States.

———

Securing Liberty. As Yale professor Akhil Reed Amar clearly describes in his book *America's Constitution*, the framers understood the need to secure liberty from the history and politics of the European nations.[42] In Europe, the aristocracy controlled the governments and militaries. Those nations each bordered hostile powers, maintained large armies and navies, and fought repeated wars over land and trade. The result was high debt for European governments, and high taxes for their people, who had few political alternatives short of armed uprising. This taxation without representation is largely what compelled the American colonies to revolt against Britain.

After the Revolution, the newly independent American states likewise each bordered competing states, had deep war debts, and faced the ongoing threat of foreign invasion and smaller-scale disputes with other states. Having rejected inherited military rule in favor of democracy, the states now faced the same problem as the Europeans: how to maintain peace and prosperity when surrounded by rivals.

For a few years, the Articles of Confederation provided loose standards for the states to work together. But the Articles provided no strong central authority to enforce agreements, and no sense of shared commitment to the confederation among most citizens. Debts between states went unpaid, disputes festered, and no serious army stood against outside threats.

In 1789, delegates from the states met to re-consider the structure of national government. The result was the Constitution, which unified the framers' philosophical goals and practical needs. Philosophically, the Constitution stated the purposes of government in the Preamble—most importantly the purpose to secure liberty. Practically, it created the mechanism for security—a strong central government with the people's authority to handle national affairs.

Further, uniting the states under a strong central government would have economic benefits. With a central government, the states would share one army and one navy instead of maintaining thirteen—a massive savings on one of the biggest expenses of all governments of the time. And the unified government could coordinate more efficiently on other common economic issues like trade and banking. Such efficiency offered the best chance for the economic and social stability that democracy and liberty would require. But security would always be the essential precondition.*

As Yale Law School Dean Harold Koh summarized, "From the very beginning, our Constitution has been obsessed with the idea of national security". Reed Amar emphatically agreed: "Our Constitution has been profoundly shaped by national security considerations, ... virtually our entire Constitution could be described, à la Koh, as 'The National Security Constitution'."[43]

And not only is securing liberty the final purpose of our government and the nation, it is also the foundation on which rest the other principles of the Preamble and the Constitution

---

* From *America's Constitution: A Biography*: "The Constitution was structured in order to create a central regime that could competently handle all affairs—whether or not economic—with Indians and foreign nations. A closely related Founding purpose was to create a central governmental structure that would handle all genuine conflicts and controversies ... that might arise between rival states, lest the aggrieved parties be tempted to take matters into their own hands and thereby imperil continental peace and prosperity."[42]

itself. Achieving them requires both national capacity and national will, so deadlocking on what efforts to pursue and how to pay for them undermines the very basis of the nation, and is a fundamental source of decline.

However, as a source of decline, this can also show the path to salvation. We can see where we've lost our way, and can also see how to regain it. Because our first principles are a mandate to secure our liberty and our happiness, we also have an unavoidable responsibility to provide the capacity and will to do so.

Capacity and will are the keys to achieving our national purpose and aspirations, as written in the Declaration and the Constitution. We, as a nation, have no alternative, legal or moral, for not working to achieve them. And the mandate is not only to do these things for ourselves, once, but to maintain them for posterity.

The challenge of deadlocked partisan politics is an existential threat to our nation, and will lead to national decline if we cannot rectify it successfully. Our founders, too, faced the need to govern in a time of divided politics and bitter disagreement. Just as they envisioned a nation thriving in perpetuity on the first principles of a just government, so can we achieve that vision.

The next chapters explore how we can do this, applying our first principles and our shared aspirations of what we know we must be, for ourselves and for the world. Working through our basic principles together, in the spirit of a nation and not just as a collection of competing groups, can return us to the democratic freedom and economic opportunity that make our aspirations a reality.

National Power—Definition and Elements

Fine words, and fine sentiment, but how can it be made concrete—how do we make our national mandate real and manifest in modern politics? The answer is Power.

As stated in the previous section, our Constitution and the nation were created to permanently secure our liberty. Yet today, a progression of distortions and polarization has pushed us to dysfunction and decline. To achieve our Constitutional purpose, we must secure liberty. And that, inescapably and by definition, requires that we rebuild and sustain our national power.

At first glance this seems so obvious as to be meaningless—clearly there can be no security without power. And yet, in that simple truth is the source of the capacity and will to enact our founding purpose. This is because we are not talking about power in the abstract, but about *national power*, a knowable characteristic of nations, with determinants that can be controlled—if a nation has the unity and will to do so.

National power is a centuries-old concept of political science. It has been studied in works as old and varied as Machiavelli's *The Prince* in 1515, with its assertion that the ends justifies the means in politics, and Thomas Hobbes's *Leviathan* in 1651, which described "a general inclination of all mankind, a perpetual and restless desire of power after power, that ceaseth only in death."[44] Theory has advanced in our own time in works by numerous scholars including Joseph Nye, Hans Morganthau, John Spanier, Robert Wendzel, Theodore Coloumbis, and James Wolfe, among others.[45] And from this work, these scholars have come to generally agree on the fundamental meaning and elements of national power.

Defined by Merriam Webster, power in the basic sense is "the ability to act or produce an effect".[46] A single definition of *national power* is not universally agreed, but common forms include "the ability to influence the behavior of others in accordance with one's own needs",[47] and "the sum of all resources available to a nation in the pursuit of national objectives".[46] Almost all definitions converge on several key ideas: ability, resources, influence, others, needs, and objectives. As a result, and based in part on the sections to follow, I will use my own definition: national power is the *capacity and will* to adapt domestically, and to influence the behavior of others internationally, in accordance with a nation's needs and objectives. Influence includes attraction, leadership, and even raw strength.

Further, modern concepts of national power generally agree that it comes from a set of fundamental elements, which have been most clearly described by Professor David Jablonsky in a 1997 paper on the subject.[48] Summarizing modern theories, he says that each of these elements of national power is either natural or social in origin. The natural elements of national power are circumstantial, and therefore are generally beyond our control: geography, climate, natural resources, and (though it is somewhat controllable) population.

The social elements are what we build over time together, the cumulative results of our lives and work. They are the national economy, politics and government, psychology, information, and the military. As the following chapters describe, national power is not merely a tool for leaders and governments to wield in foreign relations. Viewed broadly, national power is a natural result of how well the elements function, and complement each other. Because of this, power can serve as a guide to assess and manage the health of these elements, allowing us to sustain a nation that is not only more secure, but is also more just, promising a brighter future for its own citizens, and serving as a beacon to others. So understanding the elements and how they relate to each other is essential to understanding how we can harness national power in allegiance to our national purpose and principles.

In more detail, the social elements of national power are:

Economy. The economic element—the system by which goods and services are produced, sold, and bought[46]—is the primary source of national capacity. It is also a key link between the natural and social elements of power, because it includes how efficiently the population utilizes natural resources and geography for individual and collective purposes. In our modern context, the economic element includes not only manufacturing capacity, but productivity, industrial diversity, degree of innovation, trade volume, employment and price stability, and fiscal stability, among others.

Politics and government. The political-governmental element of power is determined by the form of government, and by two additional factors determining how the government functions over time. The first is the population's attitude to the government: whether it is just, fair, and representative—the Declaration's "consent of the governed". The second and related factor is government's efficiency, both in the mechanics of using resources, and more broadly in how government reacts to and addresses the changes and the issues of the day—its adaptability. Because of these multiple factors, this element of national power can also be viewed as two separate elements: politics (gaining office and making policy and law), and government (administering policy and law, and providing services).

Psychology. Related to the political element (through the consent of the governed) is the psychological element—the popular sense of nationhood. It includes national will and morale, and the degree of national integration, or sense of belonging and identification.

Information. The informational element is the most recent addition to the study of national power. It includes not just the technology and infrastructure that provide ever-increasing access to and sharing of information of all kinds, but the cultural influence or "soft power"[49] that the information can convey, from movies and music to do-it-yourself education. The scope and nature of the national media environment, including the news media, are parts of the informational element.

Military. Historically seen as the ultimate arbiter of national power, the military element is the ability to impose national will or policy by force. It describes not just the quantity and sophistication of personnel, weapons, and equipment, but also the logistics to sustain them, and the organization and leadership to employ and guide them.[50]

National Power Framework

Yet merely defining the elements, while necessary to understanding national power, is not sufficient. For national power to be a useful measure and guide, we need a framework to understand how its elements interact with and relate to each other. This is my own contribution to the field: a structural basis for applying national power in the service of our national principles and aspirations—and doing it urgently, to understand and address our current polarization and deadlock.

How the elements of national power interact with and relate to each other is not fixed or universal, but varies by political system, and by historical era. While all of the elements are relevant to any nation's power, none is sufficient alone to sustain dominant power.

To illustrate, it is useful to compare modern democracy with autocracy, two highly contrasting forms of government. Autocracies have generally sought to centralize control of the elements of power, often to the point where even the national psychology is mandated through the managed flow of information backed by the threat of force. The economy is driven by direct government control of state-owned industries, often including price and currency controls. In these systems, the political element, tightly tied to the military, is dominant.

Autocracy

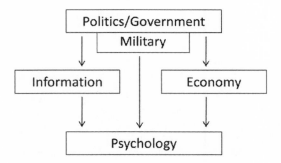

Displayed graphically, in an autocracy the political and military elements are at the top, dominating and directing the other elements. They directly control both information and the economy, and indirectly control psychology through state media and censorship, enforced by the military and/or police.

In a democracy the relationship between elements of power differs in two ways from an autocracy. First, in a democracy the elements are more balanced, so that instead of one particular element controlling the others, all the elements influence each other. Second, within this balance, the most dominant influences are circular: psychology drives politics through elections, politics drives government through policy, government sets conditions for the economy through regulation and infrastructure, and the economy drives psychology through the sense of prosperity.[†]

---

† This can be called the power cycle. Running opposite is a support cycle, in which psychology supports the economy through investment and spending, the economy supports government (and the military) through taxes, government supports politics by executing policy and law, and politics (or political leaders) support psychology through leadership decisions and a narrative about the future of the nation. While this cycle is certainly critical to national function, the power cycle by definition describes the more dominant relationships (that is, which elements direct which others). In all cases except the economy's effect on national psychology, power relationships include formal legal authority.

Democracy

The military element is part of the cycle as a component of government, and the military role during peacetime in democracies is less central than it is in autocracies, where the military often has a direct hand in enforcing civil control.

The information element, at one time the distinct institution of The Press, is now more decentralized and ubiquitous in the industrialized democracies. It can be depicted either at the center of the cycle where it connects the other elements, or more accurately all around the cycle, as an encompassing environment. This represents not only the information interaction between the other elements, but also their interaction with the outside world.

The natural elements of power (geography, climate, natural resources, and population), because they are preexisting, are a foundation on which the social elements are based.

Finally, each element contributes to either the nation's capacity or will. National capacity is determined by the economy, by scope and efficiency of government administration (including the military), and by information infrastructure. National will is determined by psychology, is enacted through politics, and is communicated by information content.

In democracies including America, all of the elements are essential, but during peacetime it is economics and politics that are most pivotal to whether national power expands or declines. They have been central to American power in the past because they are central to our ideals—the economic opportunity and political freedom to which we aspire as a nation.

Between economics and politics, however, economics is the most dominant element of national power because it forms the basis of and sustains the others. Taxes on economic activity directly fund military power. Taxes also enable political power by funding both the infrastructure of government and the services it provides. And by providing prosperity, economic power enables both psychological power and informational power: if it is broad-based, prosperity enhances psychological power by supporting morale and vested integration; and prosperity enhances informational power when that psychology and prosperity are demonstrated on the world stage.

Yet, despite the dominance of the economic element, it is the political element, including government policy, that is essential to how efficiently the economy—our capacity—operates. Politics, through economic policy and the government regulation and infrastructure established by policy, sets conditions for economic activity. And it is the current state of politics that is now exerting the biggest negative effect on national power in America, by dividing and blocking national will. This is because division and dysfunction are by definition a lack of consent and adaptability— the key factors of political power in a democracy.

In this dysfunction, party extremists refuse their consent for compromise solutions in a divided government, and create deadlock on critical issues. Under deadlock, government is unable to effectively adapt to issues or crises with new interventions. Without intervention, economic issues such as underemployment, wage stagnation and tax structure fester. As issues fester, they intensify the psychology of urgency, feeding more polarization. Yet the politics of division and extremism block our urgency from coalescing as a shared national will for reform, and the cycle of dysfunction continues.

US Power Dysfunctions, 2010s

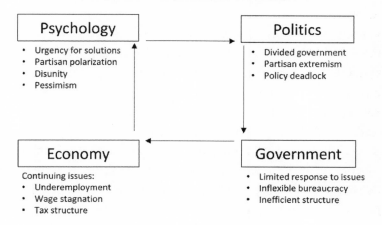

So America's national power will continue to decline unless we restore adaptable and efficient government and the consent of the governed, to re-enable our national will.

Principled Power

Long-term national power requires efficient and adaptable government that enables economic access for all citizens. This is Principled Power.

We need Principled Power because we are better than what we have let our political system become. As stated in the Preamble, our government was constituted to "secure the blessings of Liberty to ourselves, and our Posterity."

To Secure Liberty: we must expand power—the capacity and the will to enact the needs and interests of the American people. To expand our capacity and will, we need:

> *Efficient and adaptable government:* to apply resources responsibly, effectively, and decisively in the public and national interest, earning public trust and consent.

> *Economic access for all citizens:* to provide the productivity and commitment of a prosperous people.

To ourselves: To live up to our ideals, as expressed in the Constitution, and in our cultural heritage.

And our Posterity: America is the essential engine of human advance. We are the world's oldest constitutional democracy, and an engine of stability, prosperity, innovation, and justice in the world. We can assure national leadership and prosperity for another 200 years and more by deliberately focusing our aspirations for freedom and opportunity toward rebuilding and sustaining our national power.

Answering Our Challenges

We need Principled Power to motivate true reform of our distorted politics so we can effectively address our domestic challenges and external threats, now and in the future.

<u>Political Dysfunction:</u> Our national stagnation and our fears of decline are rooted in our political deadlock.

Our strength, by contrast, is rooted in our ability to adapt to changing times, within our founding principles. This ability to adapt is entirely due to our constitutional structure, and most specifically to our representative Congress, that is meant to debate our issues, and then to decide them. Principled Power states in part that national power requires adaptable government—government that can come to a decision about our most pressing issues.

Governance decisions require some compromise between the parties, which in turn requires focus on the long-term good of the nation over the good of the party. Principled Power provides that focus, allowing members of both parties to accept and eventually to lead the governance reforms we require to ensure our government works as it was designed.

Even after reforms are made, Principled Power continues to provide the focus to guide policy: a focus on expanded national power, to address the pressing domestic and international challenges that will arise in the future.

<u>Domestic challenges.</u> In our domestic affairs, we need Principled Power because while we have always had a wide range of challenges, we lack a broadly-shared philosophy of national purpose

to address them. During the Obama presidency, our debate about the size and role of government narrowed to become fundamentally about taxes and government finances—what we can and can't afford, and who benefits. Should the wealthy contribute more taxes than they do currently, to fund government programs and reduce the debt, or should we keep taxes low and cut spending?

As a result, we grossly limited our civic discussion from what we wanted our nation to be for its citizens and in history to a matter of Who Gets What. We were deadlocked on what many said were divergent visions of government. And the standoff itself was so consuming that few options were considered. In a 2012 article on the politics of scarcity, writer Mark Schmitt put it well:

> "These days, both the economic news and the bitter, deadlocked political process have made it impossible for [the President] or anyone else to paint a persuasive vision of a better future. Still one can hope that the future of American politics will lie not with those who can best manipulate scarcity and austerity to their advantage, but with those who can construct a convincing alternative."[51]

Four years later, Donald Trump won the presidency with an alternative—rejecting the post-cold-war order that had come to define liberalism: globalism's open trade and immigration, and cooperation in global treaty and regulatory organizations. His victory forced even his most strident critics to acknowledge that the liberal order was indeed failing millions of Americans, as Edward Luce and Steven Brill described. But what order can replace it—can Americans regain a generally shared vision? As columnist Ross Douthat wrote in 2018:

"Surely if there is political life after liberalism, someone will need to step forward and do what the liberal philosophers did several centuries ago—invent the new order, describe the new ideals, urge the specific transformations that future leaders might achieve."[52]

Though separated by time and circumstance, Schmitt and Douthat saw the same thing. They saw the need for a broadly shared philosophy of what the country means in the current century, and the need for a vision for a better future—of where we are going as a nation and why. Principled Power fills this need by re-focusing on our founding principles in a partisan-neutral way for the long-term; specifically, enhancing opportunity and democracy to expand national power. With Principled Power, our debates about trade, immigration, and the size and role of government are downsized to their appropriate scope—subordinate to the more fundamental question of how democracy serves citizens for long-term, broad-based economic prosperity, and the freedom and justice it allows.

<u>International challenges</u>. Internationally, American leadership is not what it was at the end of the Cold War. We face instability and failing states in the Middle East, global financial turmoil, and expanding influence by China and Russia worldwide. Any nation's international leadership comes from national power, the ability to get other nations or groups to do what they would not otherwise do. Yet today in America, dysfunction stagnates our politics and our domestic economic development, and as a result, it erodes our national power and international leadership as well.

S. J. Reynolds

In a multipolar world, America's diminished international leadership empowers non-democracies, emboldens dictators, and undermines stability and security. It ultimately degrades markets and economic development, which rely on certainty, predictability, open access, and the rule of law.

Principled Power orients us to the bottom line of international relations: power prevails in the long run in the hands of nations able and willing to adapt to and to lead changing conditions. And as wary as we Americans are about concentrated power, and as reluctant as we might be to pursue it as a final goal, there are and always will be others around the world such as the large autocracies who seek power deliberately and aggressively, and largely against our interests.

So internationally, the long term choice before us is whether to expand power ourselves in a restored, adaptable, and benevolent Constitutional system, or to cede it to others. We can and must restore our national power, for the sake of not only ourselves, our neighbors, and our children, but also as an example to others around the world.

Three

POWER POLITICS

To expand our national power, our first job is to reform the distortions in our electoral system, to restore function to our politics and government.

To restore and even to expand our national power, we must become capable again of shared national will. This requires government that is efficient and adaptable, acting decisively in the public interest and the voters' interests, instead of deadlocking on party interests or special interests. And to do this we have to first end the ways that special interests have warped and distorted our electoral system to accumulate power and influence for themselves.

Electoral Finance Reform

The most fundamental distortion, and the biggest insult to the Constitution and to our nation, is what we have allowed to happen to our system of election funding. Certainly, the framers did not have modern election funding in mind when developing and ratifying the Constitution, so we don't know whether they would consider it Constitutional. However, it is hard to imagine that they would endorse the type of anonymous political speech we now have, or endorse political power gathered and wielded by anonymous moneyed factions. And yet, these are currently sanctioned by the Supreme Court through the *Citizens United* decision, and have increasingly become major factors in American elections.

Any citizen who hasn't considered what this means should think about it for a moment: our national elections are now massively influenced by large donations from sources that can remain anonymous. These donors can loudly promote any candidate or any position that will benefit them, without it being directly traced back to them. So-called super PACs and 501.c.4 social welfare groups allow individuals and corporations to anonymously contribute unlimited donations to support "issues", which are easily word-smithed in ads to clearly promote individual candidates for election, usually by attacking the opponent.

And because corporations are not restricted from this system of anonymous speech, large companies and government contractors funnel money through lobbyists to support candidates the same way. As a result, wealthy individuals, corporations and lobbying groups, through their donations to fund political ads, get outsized access and political voice through elected officials, and get decision power over our national laws. And politicians who don't go along with this system, whether incumbents or challengers, see their ad funding go to others who will.

The vast majority of American citizens on all parts of the political spectrum have a fundamental interest in ending these special arrangements. The most urgent and important action to reform these distortions is for voters to ***insist on the end of unlimited political donations, and of anonymous or undisclosed donations.***

Americans are justifiably proud of the virtuous intent of our Constitutional design, and of our rule of law. We have checks and balances, due process of law, and we can get a fair hearing in court. The idea that our political system can be called *corrupt* is so foreign, that in all the discussion and debate about money in politics and campaign finance, the word is rarely used. Instead we think of corruption as paying cold cash to an official for an immediate political favor or result. We might not be quite there, but we are closer than some might want to admit.

Unlimited funding of anonymous political speech is wrong because it is an affront to several of our Constitutional principles. It violates *Justice*: one person, one vote is severely hindered by unlimited donations, and anonymity in speech prevents any candidate from being able to face a political accuser. It violates *a more perfect Union*: it legitimizes pay for influence. And perhaps in the future it could violate *Tranquility*: how long will people peacefully stand for this? We urgently need to reform this system before it gets worse.

This process of reform will be extremely challenging, with the status quo protected by large political and media funding. While there may be several paths to take, any real reform requires voter dedication over several years to accomplish two essential goals: 1) conferring Constitutional power on Congress to enact reforms of anonymous corporate political speech, and then 2) enacting the reforms themselves.

<u>Unaccountable Speech</u>. The first goal is the most important, because Congress lost the power to control corporate speech in the 2010 *Citizens United* case. In it, the Supreme Court said in essence that Congress does not have the Constitutional power to limit political speech such as paid advertisements by "associations of citizens", including corporations. The immediate effect is that no laws can now be made to stop super PACs or social welfare groups from using unlimited donations from corporations, lobby groups, and wealthy individuals for speaking about "issues"—thinly veiled campaign ads.

The broader effect, however, is to cement massive additional Constitutional rights for corporations and lobby groups, protecting them in applying their vast financial resources to support candidates. The individual citizens of our country, through Congress, must have the power to control this form of paid political influence. Unless the Supreme Court reverses its ruling from *Citizens United*, Congress will only regain this power of control through a Constitutional amendment, requiring widespread citizen support to enact.

Generating this support will be an extraordinarily daunting undertaking, requiring in part an absolute crystal clarity of principle, so soon after a Supreme Court ruling. In the ruling, the majority of justices generally said that associations of citizens, including super PACs, corporations, and lobbyists, have the right to freedom of speech under the First Amendment. This right means Congress cannot limit associations in making advertisements about political issues.

How can citizens answer this? What can we say against freedom of speech—is there any principle as fundamental? Yes, while political speech is a right, citizens must still be *accountable* for their political speech. Simply put, anonymous speech—and especially corporate-paid anonymous speech—is not what the First Amendment exists to protect. Because even if we were to accept that money spent on political advertising is equivalent to political speech, and is protected by the First Amendment, we also have limits on free speech, like any right, when it is intended to harm others.

The First Amendment does not protect us from shouting "Fire" in a crowded auditorium, nor should it protect anyone from using anonymous donations to a super PAC for ads that say anything to defeat an electoral opponent. Such donors are not accountable for their "speech", and have brazenly worked to buy electoral results and the consequent influence with their candidates once in office.

Skeptics might reasonably ask where this principle of accountability comes from—is it written in the Declaration or Constitution? It is written *on* them: the founders and framers didn't tack anonymous flyers to trees or paint anonymous slogans on walls when they created the Declaration and the Constitution; rather, they personally signed both of our great charters, in the Declaration even pledging "our lives, our fortunes, our sacred honor".

While passing an amendment for reform is a difficult and lengthy process, and requires grassroots support, Principled Power stands as a critical asset of national will. Simply put, Principled Power can popularize the fact that adaptable government is key to our national power. This in turn can focus bipartisan support on what is at stake in election funding reform, to rally voters from both sides of the aisle to the fundamental cause of an amendment.

Anonymous power by corporations and wealthy individuals has polarized Congress to a standoff that specifically benefits the donors. In this standoff, the big donors serve as tiebreakers, with inordinate power to end obstructions or broker deals that are favorable to them. If the legislature only works when corporations and the wealthy allow, the nation will only adapt as it suits these special interests, severely endangering the benefits of broad economic access and prosperity.

How will Congress react to a widespread call for an amendment? Do its members want these reforms, or do they want to maintain the status quo?

Regardless of their personal feelings about reform, politicians want to win elections. So initially, the majority of Congress will defend the status quo against outside voices and the few internal reformers. In the end however, Congress and the parties themselves will follow the political incentives, shifting positions to support reform as soon as there is sufficient voter demand. It will be a lengthy battle, but we as individual citizens have no alternative if we hope to preserve our democracy.

The Danger of Corporate Political Rights. Setting aside the argument of accountable speech, what is the problem with corporations having political power? If corporations create jobs and drive the economy, isn't it appropriate for them to have a say in our government and politics?

Giving political rights to corporations is a dangerous practice because it fundamentally flies in the face of the nation's first principles as established by We The People: that "... governments are instituted among men, and derive their just powers from the consent of the governed." Our government is by, for, and of the people, not for corporations or anything else for that matter, and it is important to examine this in more detail.

———

I was about a year into my first job in the private sector, as an associate manager in pharmaceuticals, after leaving Army active duty in the late 90's. Looking over the accounting records one day for a project I'd been assigned, I saw that the company was making its sales target in recent years with an annual "buy-in"—negotiating with our major wholesale customers to buy much more of our product than the market actually demanded. As a result, our company's sales looked good on Wall Street. When I asked about it, I was told "that's the way we've always done it, that's just how it is. It's normal." Since none of this was related to my assigned project, I accepted the explanation and continued with my work. A year later, the company was indicted for securities fraud for this scheme, and settled with a large fine. No executives went to jail, and only the shareholders' investments suffered for management's shady dealings.

———

Corporations in the broadest sense are legal forms of organization that exist to pool resources and limit individual risk for accomplishing a specific purpose. Historically in Europe, rulers or governments chartered a very few individual corporations to accomplish specific national objectives. Examples would include running a colony overseas to extract resources for a profit, like the British East India Company, or building and operating a canal or bridge, like the Chesapeake and Ohio Canal Company.

In modern America by contrast, corporations are created freely every day, with a one-page application, for the general purpose of making money. As rudimentary as it sounds, this is the key to the issue: corporations exist to make a profit. Sure, in recent years we have the growing trend of "corporate social responsibility", and we have rising numbers of companies like *Newman's Own* who donate their profits to charity.

But make no mistake about two essential truths. First, any corporation's primary loyalty is to making a profit by competitive success. This is because without profit, there can be no corporate citizenship and responsibility—those things are only for corporations that win in the market. And second, corporations pay huge sums to the top managers who accomplish the profit job best, and they fire the people who don't. Corporate leaders talk about (and in most cases truly believe in) the value of social responsibility, but their paychecks depend on profit first.

And so, when there is any legal opportunity to protect and increase profit, the corporate executives generally do it. And these opportunities include lobbying the government and politicians, and helping to elect those candidates who promise favorable legislation.

Even more so, executives are legally bound to do this, because boards of directors have a binding fiduciary responsibility to represent the interests of investors in making a profit. To do it, the boards hire executives and pay them to accomplish that one thing first. Corporations are generally led and populated by good people, but the corporations exist to make money.

All that said, the corporate form has indeed accomplished great things for the United States. Corporations create employment, materials, products, and yes, profits for shareholders, including anyone with a 401k plan. Also, American corporations have been and remain the engine of American military dominance since WWII. They create and provide not only more and ultimately better planes, ships, tanks, and munitions, but the superior logistical capacity to transport and supply them.

But corporations and their attendant industrial activities have always had costs, which we have worked hard to manage: pollution, resource depletion, labor-management conflict, and social change. And now we are acutely feeling one of the most consequential costs, which also needs to be managed: political influence. Corporations, intended as a tool to create prosperity for citizens, are becoming citizens in their own right. As affirmed by the Supreme Court in 2010 in the *Citizen's United* case, corporations now have a legalized voice in our national politics and government.

And corporations are legally bound to use this voice in government and politics just like they use any other asset or tool: to increase their own profits in any way possible. In government affairs, that means using their vast resources to advocate for laws and policies in their own profit interests above anything else.

And what is good for a single corporation's or industry's profits in the short term is not likely to be what is good for the country as a whole in the long term—remember pollution, resource depletion, labor-management conflict, and social change. And that, at the end of the day, is the danger of legalized corporate citizenship.

Our first principles state that it is people that have equal rights, and that government exists to secure those rights for people. *We the People* seek life, liberty, and the pursuit of happiness; corporations seek profit, and are bound to do everything legal to get it. Corporations are economic tools. They are not people, they are not citizens, and they should not have the political rights of citizens.

As people we have not only hopes and dreams, but also vast capacity for empathy and compassion. Most importantly perhaps, we have the vision and the ability to invest and sacrifice today for a better life and world tomorrow, for ourselves and our future generations. We are allowing political power for corporations at our great peril—if we continue with it, we will soon be a republic no more. If it hasn't happened already.

———

As the Constitutional voice of the people, Congress must have the power to regulate the terms of moneyed political speech, period. Without this power and the attendant reforms, any person or corporation retains the right to pay to influence elections anonymously through super PACs and social welfare groups. As a result, government by, for, and of the people is in serious danger of perishing from the earth.

However, securing regulatory power for Congress over corporate political speech is only half the battle. The other half, to be waged in parallel, is to enact the electoral finance reforms themselves. The case for, and recommended design of these reforms has been expertly described by the political scholars Thomas Mann and Norman Ornstein in *It's Even Worse Than It Looks* (2012),[53] and this section directly applies and endorses many of their recommendations for reform.

Several reforms are needed here, and if taken piecemeal, these reforms are likely to be too varied and arcane to maintain the public's attention. Together, however, they can form a more easily understood package for reform—an Electoral Reform Act. The critical reforms are:

- A law eliminating super PACs and leadership PACs. Both of these mechanisms brazenly skirt existing laws intended to provide transparency in election funding. The PACs are designed to allow unlimited, anonymous donations to support "social issues", and are not supposed to support candidates, parties, or to coordinate with campaigns. However, they easily do all of these things using broad loopholes in the laws, and are a major insult to the principle of accountable political speech. They should be outlawed, period.
- A law forbidding the acceptance of contributions for a candidacy or political party from organizations that lobby or contract with the government. Lobbying and contracting are important functions in our government. However, lobbyists and contractors should not be allowed to financially support candidates for federal elected office, period.
- A law requiring any independent spending group to disclose large donors, and to reveal large donor identities directly and immediately in political ads.
- More stringent oversight of the executive agencies and departments that are charged with enforcing the disclosure and anti-coordination laws that are already on the books. Enforcement of the law is not political persecution if enforcement is done evenhandedly, as it must be to support our governance.

S. J. Reynolds

What can individual voters do to initiate such broad reforms against such entrenched interests? To begin, voters must join electoral reform groups such as IssueOne.org, NoLabels.org, and Bipartisanpolicy.org. And voters must ask their Congressional representatives to **support the elimination of super PACs and anonymous political spending.** It is deceptively simple, but it will let Congress and the parties know where voters stand on this straightforward issue in defense of our democracy.

Even this simple act will quickly meet resistance from the lucrative industry of political consultants, lobbyists, and the top funders that support them as a way to retain influence. However, with sufficient grassroots support, a tipping point will come when the main parties recognize the prize for endorsing reform: capture of the political center, possibly for years to come. Ultimately, the reforms will have the inevitability of women's suffrage in the 1920's, or the civil rights reforms of the 1960's. Only with reform will representatives answer to their real constituent voters as the Constitution intends, instead of to companies or to targeted interests, as we have let happen in recent years.

Do the Right Thing. To build national power, we must have government that is efficient and adaptable, enabling public trust and consent. Government cannot be efficient or adaptable while electoral finance is distorted to favor moneyed anonymous speech. These distortions allow paid political influence by wealthy individuals, corporations, and groups whose interests are not representative of the electorate as a whole.

There are only a few things that each of us as individual voters

66

needs to do to effect real change in electoral finance, listed below and as part of the final conclusion at the end of the book.

Collectively, we must reform our electoral financing in accordance with our principles of accountable speech. Our most important collective action is to support *an amendment or equivalent Constitutional authority* for Congress to regulate political speech by corporations and associations, including super PACs. Once this is done, we must push Congress for an *Electoral Reform Act*, including eliminating super PACs and campaign contributions by lobbyists and government contractors, and tightening and enforcing contribution limits and rules on disclosure.

As individuals, while there are many things we each might do, the first and most important is to simply ask our officeholders and candidates to support eliminating super PACs and unlimited political donations. The next thing is to join and support the independent groups (IssueOne.org, NoLabels.org, and Bipartisanpolicy.org) that advocate for these electoral finance reforms; and to talk openly about our intent to vote on reform issues above all others. Without reform, all of our other debates in politics and policy merely prolong and intensify our dysfunction.

Voting Practices Reform

As large and important as electoral finance reform is, it can still only address part of the distortions in our electoral system. To be truly effective, reform must also include an end to the distorted voting practices that have further encouraged extremism, obstructionism, and the government deadlock that results. As with finance reform, several specific measures are needed, and would be best packaged along with the finance reforms in a comprehensive Electoral Reform Act.

The voting distortions that have combined to enable extremism and deadlock often go back decades, and can be seemingly innocuous when viewed individually. Combined, however, they create relatively safe congressional seats and encourage politically extreme positions by incumbents and challengers alike. Like the campaign finance reforms outlined in the previous section, these voting distortions are also well-described by Mann and Ornstein in *It's Even Worse Than It Looks*, and the remainder of this section likewise applies and endorses many of their recommendations.

There are two groups of voting distortions: how we conduct voting in federal elections, and how the Senate conducts its internal voting. None of these practices are mandated by the Constitution; they have developed over time to manage the respective processes. However, in recent decades the effects of these separate practices have combined to create the unintended consequences of extremism and deadlock we see today.

Not only are we Constitutionally free to reform these practices, but it is our Constitutional duty to do so, in support of basic principles of democratic process. Consider these basic ideas which, while not specified in the Constitution, are nonetheless straightforward first principles of what fair voting practices entail.

- Congressional representatives should be elected by a general geographic locality, not by a custom party district. Custom party districts promote divisions within a city or region. Party-blind districts promote engagement and build communities by involving multiple viewpoints in each district.

- All citizens should vote, or at least have the opportunity to do so easily.
- Primary elections are a useful mechanism to narrow a large field of candidates for general elections. Primaries should not prejudice the general election by providing an advantage to the most politically extreme candidate from each party to advance to the general election.
- For voting in the Senate, the majority should rule, with a provision for the minority to voice extreme opposition in the most exceptional circumstances.

In opposition to these general principles of democratic process, relatively minor distortions have combined so that primaries favor more politically extreme candidates to stand for general election, and the most partisan voters are over-represented on election days. In the Senate, a minority of extremists on either side can effectively block action by the majority. In more detail:

- Congressional redistricting, which is Constitutionally mandated following each 10-year census, currently has few restrictions against partisan manipulation in most states. State politicians are able to design and negotiate custom-drawn districts to favor one party or the other. As a result, internal district politics favor more ideologically pure or extreme candidates and incumbents.
- Election Day is Tuesday, mandated by an 1845 law to make it convenient for farmers to get to the polls between church on Sunday and market days at the end of the week. Today, this convention makes it highly *in*-convenient

for most working people to attend the polls, and therefore favors the more dedicated voters (who tend to be more ideologically extreme) to attend the polls and be represented.

- Most primary elections are open only to the members of the party holding the primary. This alone favors the selection of more ideologically pure candidates within the party, and is further amplified by the greater likelihood of the ideologically-dedicated to vote in primary elections.
- Partisan abuse of the once-arcane rule of the Senate filibuster is rampant, requiring a super-majority of 60% of Senators to override a filibuster and decide any major issue. This effectively deadlocks the upper house of our legislative branch in our present era of 50-50 divided government.

To counter these distortions, an Electoral Reform Act needs to adopt Mann and Ornstein's well-researched and balanced reforms:

- Independent redistricting: all states delegate redistricting authority to independent redistricting committees, with clear standards for partisan fairness in selecting members, and for political blindness in the redistricting.
- Weekend elections with mandatory attendance: voting noon on Saturday until noon on Sunday, for maximum convenience regarding work schedules and religious observance. (And if we are ever really serious about universal voting, attendance at polls can be required by law, with a minor $20 fine and flexible options such as early voting.)

As Mann and Ornstein describe, this system has worked for decades in democratic Australia, with voting participation at 80 – 90%, even in lower-profile election events.

- Open primaries: institute so-called Top Two Vote Getter (TTVG) primaries such as California's. In these, candidates of all parties are listed on the primary ballot, with the first and second place winners advancing to the general election for a run-off. As Mann and Ornstein explain, this better aligns the function of primaries with the function of elections: to narrow the field of candidates based on positions instead of on their adherence to party purity.

- Filibuster reform: only one filibuster should be allowed in the Senate per bill, with the burden on the minority party to demonstrate any extraordinary opposition by continuously holding the floor for debate. With such a reform, the minority can make its stand clear, but the majority ultimately rules, as the Constitution clearly states. By effectively returning majority rule to the Senate, this will remove the main weapon of obstructionists, which will moderate partisan rhetoric and positions along the way. As a result, the Senate will be able to act on our national issues, greatly revitalizing our power of adaptable government.

Through these relatively simple reforms, we can eliminate the distortions in our voting practices that favor extremist positions on both ends of the spectrum, and the government deadlock that results. With these reforms, political leaders will need to engage with and appeal to a wider spectrum of beliefs among their constituents. And leaders will be much less likely penalized in elections for working with their elected colleagues across the political spectrum to solve problems and to meet challenges.

Combined with the reduced influence of special interests through basic reforms in electoral funding, these measures will restore greater function to Congress. Ultimately, these will again allow our nation to create a shared will for adapting to our challenges, in allegiance to our beliefs and to the Constitution.

B y Principled Power, national power for America, as for any nation, depends on efficient and adaptable government and on political consent—all essential for shared will. These are today crippled by dysfunction, polarization, and deadlock created by accumulated distortions of our electoral system, and maintained by the interests of wealthy campaign donors, lobby groups, corporations, and their candidates who all hold great power in times of deadlock. Ending polarization and deadlock restores decision making and consent.

We can restore efficient, adaptable government and political consent by two actions, the first of which is to pass an amendment to the Constitution to control anonymous political speech. The second is an Electoral Reform Act to control unlimited donations, and to eliminate the distortions in our voting practices that enable deadlock by favoring extremist positions.

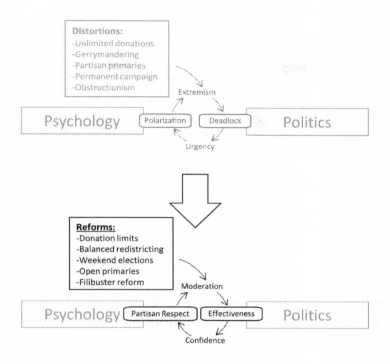

By restoring adaptability and consent, we restore shared will: the political function that allows us to create capacity. These are the cornerstones of our power to secure liberty for ourselves and our posterity.

So it bears repeating: working through our basic principles together, in the spirit of a nation and not just as a collection of competing groups, will get us to the democracy, prosperity, and greatness that make our aspirations a reality. We can and must restore the capacity and will for our national power, for the sake of not only ourselves, our neighbors, and our children, but also as an example to others around the world.

<u>Do the Right Thing</u>. Like the previous section, there are only a few things that each of us as individual voters needs to do to effect real change in electoral practices, which are also listed in the final conclusion at the end of the book.

Collectively, we must reform electoral practices beyond electoral finance, and in accordance with our principles of fair voting. This means demanding that Congress, our parties, and our states support an Electoral Reform Act for balanced and party-blind redistricting reforms, weekend elections, and open primaries. And we must demand reform of Senate filibuster practices.

And, as stated previously, the most important actions we can take as individuals are to write our representatives in support of these reforms, to join and support the independent groups that advocate for these reforms, and to talk openly about our intent to vote on reform issues above all others. Without reform, any other political effort merely prolongs and intensifies our dysfunction.

Four

Government has a central role in our national power, shaping economic capacity based on political will. Because we are a republic, the government answers to the people, and reflects who we are by what we demand of it. Managed by principle, our government can be great without being out of control.

As Principled Power recognizes, our first principles support building long-term national power. The previous chapter addressed Principled Power's application in electoral politics, which is a key expression of our national will. While we certainly need electoral reform to expand our power, it is not enough—we also need reform in government. This chapter addresses Principled Power's applications in government—both how government works, and what policies it makes. Both of these determine whether government builds or erodes our national power.

This is because national power depends on *both* the capacity of economic strength *and* the will of a political system that is efficient and trusted, and government is the link between them. Consider: while economics affects politics most directly through national psychology, by the voters' satisfaction with their prosperity and opportunity, politics affects economics through government—how much government costs, and what economic policies government makes. For better or worse, government has a critical role: translating will to capacity.

So critical, in fact, that the question of government's size and role has now become a defining issue of our politics, and of our deadlock. To break this deadlock, we must agree on answers to two fundamental questions. First, what is the just role of government in modern terms, according to our first principles? And second, how can government be less expensive, and yet more effective? If we can agree on the answers, we can have a vision of government that is shared more broadly than today.

This chapter shows how we can not only fix our deadlock on the role of government, but also strengthen the economy to create broader opportunity. They key is a new mechanism for government policy-making that is simple and effective, and applies our fundamental principles in support of our national power.

The Role of Government—First Principles

We turn first to the size and role of government. Because the role of government is one of the most fundamental debates underlying our current political deadlock, we must again rely on our first principles as a starting point to address it—and specifically we must again turn to the Constitution. The Constitution created our government to:

- *Establish justice*: that is, making, administering, and adjudicating laws, to the ends of providing fair redress.
- *Insure domestic Tranquility*: maintaining civil order—requiring that government protect rights to minimize grievances.
- *Provide for the common defense*: maintaining national security.
- *Promote the general Welfare*: not merely providing a safety net for the vulnerable, but managing the public goods on which we all rely.
- *Secure the Blessings of Liberty*: protecting our rights and freedoms from loss—for any reason, including by the distortions that create our current political dysfunction.

This is the philosophy of what our government was designed to do at its founding, so this must be our starting point in considering the role of government in the new century.

To create a shared vision from that point, we must hold proudly to two fundamental facts. The first is that our nation is largely defined by the existence, basic structure, and centrality of the federal government. So, while only a very small but vocal minority suggests there should be no federal government or only the shell of a government, it has no Constitutional legitimacy in a discussion of how the United States should function.

The second fact is that the federal government was established to accomplish several purposes, as listed in the Preamble, and

above. Further, these purposes are self-evidently broad in scope
and never-ending. So a shared vision of government must begin
from the point that the federal government must exist, must be
central, and is the active, leading agent for accomplishing the purpose of the United States. These first principles form the philosophical foundation of the role of government in America.

<u>"The general Welfare:" Public Good</u>. While it is vital to use the
fundamental principles of the Constitution as our foundation,
it is also important to build on that foundation based on our
advancing knowledge. And from this, we know that governments
are essential to manage *public goods*: interests and resources that
no other individual or market has the incentive to manage, but
from which everyone benefits. This is the Constitution's charge to
"promote the general Welfare".

Common examples of public goods include a strong economy,
public infrastructure, defense, fundamental scientific research, and
a clean environment. Yet foremost among these for our national
power is a strong economy. And critically, most western democracies, including America, manage the economy by regulation.

Here of course is a fundamental difference between conservative and liberal philosophy, and a source of our deadlock: the
extent to which government should regulate the economy. In general, conservatives feel that the free market is the most efficient
way to provide a strong economy, and to manage many other
public goods. They note government's inherently political nature,
its lack of efficiency and quality in the absence of competitive
pressure, and the bureaucratic burden in time and money of excessive regulation.

By contrast, liberals generally feel that government is essential to manage certain public goods and services that the market does not have an incentive to manage, and also to protect against the potential excesses of unrestrained capitalism. Liberals are willing to accept some limitations to personal freedom, such as taxes and regulatory requirements, for these extra protections.

<u>Regulated Markets Are American</u>. Most experts and historians believe that neither one pure approach nor the other (free market only or government-controlled only) is most beneficial in every case. What we have evolved instead is a system of regulated markets.

Within this system, the federal and state governments have worked to create an effective balance of regulation in each sector of the economy and society. The amount of regulation can vary widely in each sector, and it can also change over time within a sector. Managing that balance is complex, but we live in a complex world, and we have created and refined systems and agencies to manage the complexities of these markets. (The question is the efficiency and the cost of these agencies, discussed shortly—can they be both better and less expensive?)

Setting aside the complexities, most people can reasonably accept that some regulation is needed in practically every market to protect the public and the environment. Sensible regulation, for example, keeps fly-by-night companies from selling ineffective or dangerous medicines. It keeps companies from dumping toxic waste into fields, rivers, and the air. And it ensures that fishing operations leave enough of each species behind to reproduce for the following year's catch. So, in promoting essential protections, liberals defend an important fundamental concept.

S. J. Reynolds

The ongoing challenge is to balance the regulation with economic vibrancy. For example, de-regulation of trucking and airlines in the 1980's has generally made those industries more efficient, allowing cheaper goods and services for consumers. In promoting economic freedom, conservatives defend an important fundamental concept.

The point is that no one size fits all; rather, when our system works as it was originally conceived, our elected representatives should be able to find and periodically adjust the right balance for the national good. Balance is essential.

The problem with regulation is not whether it is appropriate or effective; we need regulation, and it is effective, for the reasons above. The problem is that the system is not currently working as it was conceived—a problem that can be fixed, as described shortly. Yet the essential principle remains that regulated markets are American: they are fundamental to how our nation balances its first principles of ensuring the public good, while also remaining the land of opportunity and free enterprise.

As stated before, our foremost public good is a strong and sustainable national economy. Effective government does not create economic prosperity and power by itself, but it has an essential role in maintaining the conditions for economic power. Economic power is the engine of national power, and it must be managed sustainably, where the public good is balanced with profit. And in particular, these public goods must include economic access for all citizens, for the long-term good of the entire nation.

The essential challenge, however, is for government to do this at a size and efficiency that the population will tolerate long-term.

Enacting Our Principles of Government

The essential principles of American government are strong. And yet our trust in government—the consent of the governed—has fallen precipitously for a large segment of Americans. A poll of satisfaction with the US system of government and how well it works fell from over 60% in the early 2000s to under 40% in 2012, where it has remained.[54] Another clear demonstration of mistrust, long before President Trump's election, is that millions supported multiple government shutdowns during the Obama administration, rather than willingly increase government's funding. Most of those millions, it is fair to say, were less protesting government's fundamental existence, than they were protesting government's inefficiency, and the costs it imposes on businesses and taxpayers in time and money.

Government inefficiency, described in the quotes from Zakaria and Fukuyama in the first chapter, causes public mistrust, which leads to less government funding. Less government funding then worsens government inefficiency and dysfunction in a downward cycle.

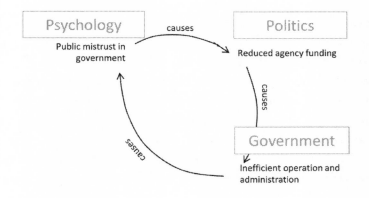

This was certainly not how government was intended to function at our founding. However, like our electoral system, the function of government has become distorted over time, becoming burdensome and untrusted enough to threaten the basis of our national power. Fortunately, also like our electoral system, we can reform government according to our principles, and restore national power.

Our government needs three major reforms to align it to the principles by which it was conceived, and to build national power in the modern age. These reforms are the basis of Principled Power. They are reforms of:

- Government bureaucracy and regulation—because power requires efficient and adaptable government.
- Economic policy—because power requires a fully accessible economy.
- Policy-making systems—because Principled Power requires a mechanism for action.

Reform 1: National Power Requires Efficient Government.

<u>Government Out of Control</u>. Breaking the negative cycle of government inefficiency requires not only political reform to reduce deadlock in Congress, but also administrative reform.

In particular, administrative reform must fix a government, and specifically a regulatory structure, that a large segment of the population sees as increasingly out-of-control, self-serving, and ultimately insidious. The charge is not baseless. Almost all

American adults experience at various times a federal government bureaucracy that is burdensome, confusing, and unreasoning.

In our personal lives, we most commonly experience the burden of bureaucracy in filing federal income tax paperwork. In our work lives, dealing with government bureaucracy can be exponentially more pronounced for those working in highly regulated industries such as healthcare, food preparation, finance, and construction. On a regular basis, whether in large multinational corporations or in small family businesses, business owners and managers must file paperwork and undergo inspections to demonstrate compliance with long lists of highly detailed specifications, or be fined, shut down, or possibly prosecuted.

This system imposes significant economic costs on businesses and individuals not only in the time and effort to remain compliant, but also in the taxes we pay for the large bureaucracy to monitor and inspect us. It is perfectly understandable that so many people feel, in the words of Ronald Reagan, that "government is not the solution to our problems, government is the problem." And yet, as most people realize, we can't simply have no regulation or government agencies—without them, there would be no control on pollution, on food and drug safety, on what banks do with our savings—and the list goes on.

So, this is the question of the role of our government: is there an alternative to burdensome bureaucracy on the one hand, or economic anarchy on the other? Can government agencies be smaller—less costly—and yet more effective? The answer is yes: smaller yet more effective government is absolutely achievable—and long overdue—and principles are essential to making it happen.

To understand why and how, it is important to understand why and how our systems of government administration and regulation were originally designed over 200 years ago, and how they continue to operate. The fact is that the basic design of government operation and regulation is badly outdated and inefficient, and can be greatly improved by a deliberate modernization program, and by application of fundamental principles.

As described by legal thinker Philip Howard in his important 2014 book *The Rule of Nobody*, the primary cause of bureaucratic inefficiency in government is that the concept of the rule of law has gone too far. Essentially, the well-meaning idea of government by a rule of law—a final authority that nobody is above—was originally established in the early 1800s to prevent tyranny and corruption from taking root in government. To do this, government was designed to run by objective black-and-white rules that left minimal room for officials to use their positions for personal gain.

The downside in modern times, worsening every year, is that government is structured to perform all its functions automatically, by dense clockwork of minute rules, regulations, and paperwork. It is designed to replace judgment and flexibility with a rule-bound bureaucracy that is, by intention, mindless and inflexible. In removing human influence and judgment from government regulation and administration, we remove human creativity, adaptability, and passion as well. The bureaucracy is heartless as well as mindless—indeed out of human control.

Such a system never fully achieves what it intends, because fixed rules for every eventuality are impossible. And yet despite only partial benefit, there are costs we know too well. The first cost is economic: what we pay in taxes for a large bureaucracy to monitor compliance with large volumes of rules, and what we pay in time and paperwork to demonstrate compliance.

And yet, higher than the economic costs of inefficiency are the political costs—our diminished trust and consent in government and its roles. Loss of trust and consent is a primary driver of our partisan deadlock over the critical issue of the role of government and how to pay for it. Simply put, a large proportion of voters now flatly refuses—not unreasonably—any tax increases to support a government they see as inefficient and burdensome.

The result however is that by effectively halting government's funding and its decision-making, the deadlock is slowing or stopping any national response to almost every new issue, challenge, or threat that we face. If power is the ability to affect our environment, then inability to respond—deadlock—is the loss of power. This demonstrates Francis Fukuyama's point from the previous section: inefficient government diminishes consent and creates deadlock. Deadlock prevents efforts at reform, hardening a cycle of decline.

So, this is our dilemma. Despite these costs, and the frustration it breeds, reacting to government bureaucracy by merely shrinking government or starving it of funding is an example of cutting off our noses to spite our faces. It fails to correct the underlying mechanisms of mindless bureaucracy, leaving the part that remains as bureaucratic as before, but unable to perform its required functions as well. The worst of all worlds.

Regaining Control of Government. To productively address uncontrolled government bureaucracy, we have to again return to first principles. We The People established the Constitution and the government. Government by, for, and of the people means that there is no Us vs. Them regarding government—there is only Us. Self-government is a responsibility, and therefore any failures of government design and structure are our own. If we believe our government is out of control, it is squarely up to us as citizens to repair it, because scrapping it is not an option. A strong and effective government of a powerful nation does not have to be burdensome on individuals or businesses. Effective government can and should be an enabler and an accelerator for individual prosperity and therefore for national power.

This is where principle comes in. For government to function as an accelerator, we need a balance between the one extreme of no regulation and the other extreme of excessive, mindless regulation. This balance, as Philip Howard describes, can be achieved by replacing volumes of detailed rules and specifications with fewer yet broader principles and objectives, providing high-level guidance to leaders who are accountable to achieve it according to their creativity, passion, and resources.

This is a well-known and long-used practice in the private sector, which in the government can empower leaders to make active, useful choices to provide public services that are efficient and adaptable.

We can achieve the ends of regulation for the "general welfare", and the ends of government administration overall by a reformed system that simplifies government structure, and harnesses human creativity to manage the public good efficiently and effectively, instead of implementing volumes of minute rules.

Despite the clear advantages however, such a change will not be easy. Managing government effectiveness and reforming it as an accelerator will certainly require deliberate attention and effort, including the involvement and leadership of Congress. This will take time, and we will need to stay focused on it throughout.

But it can be done, and the second half of this chapter describes how. Regardless, the existence and form of our government defines who we are as a nation, and the government has a critical role to play in who we will be in the future. Government can be simultaneously smaller, less costly, and yet more effective. Government must be an accelerator for our economic prosperity; otherwise it is baggage, or a brake. Managed with more intention, we can ensure it is an accelerator.

Reform 2: National Power Requires Full Economic Access

Economic Policy Needs a New Approach. The US and world economies have been fragile at best since the financial crisis of 2008. The few major nations with any economic growth since then—the US, Germany, and China—carry heavy economic baggage that persistently threatens to overwhelm growth. But more importantly, our governments have few economic tools remaining to respond to a new downturn. The ammo is spent, so to speak, which means that business as usual for economic policy is increasingly dangerous, and it is important to understand this in more detail.

Overseas, Germany's strong and efficient economy is essentially guaranteeing the solvency of other indebted European countries. If these countries default on their large debts, it will put overwhelming stress on not only Germany's economy and banks, but on banks worldwide. In China the economy also carries high debt, which Chinese companies had used to finance many years of growth. But slowing growth calls into question whether the companies can keep paying their loans.

And in the US, despite the official end of the Great Recession and its high unemployment, growth and prosperity come from corporate profits, which mostly benefits corporate employees and investors. And even this renewed growth has been weak by historical standards, never too far from being overwhelmed by high debt carried by millions of households and by the government.

So, even if politics was not deadlocked and government was not inefficient, the country has few resources to weather new shocks. This is because the economy itself is fragile, and government's tools for managing crises are already in full use to keep us moving out of the last crisis. If there is another crisis, whether it starts at home or overseas, there is little the US government can do to respond.

The main tools the government uses to react to crises are government spending projects, interest rates, and the money supply. Spending projects provide the economy with additional fuel (though at the cost of more government debt), higher interest rates apply the brakes, and money supply can do both. Whether we think these tools have been used wisely or not in the past, how they work is clear and well-known. Also well-known is the fact that these tools are in full use already, leaving us in a dangerous spot.

To understand why, it is effective to think about the economy like a car, or better yet a long-haul truck. While the economy, like a truck, is a highly complex system, its speed is a result of the strength of the engine, the weight of the truck, and the combination of gas and braking. But it also depends on the steepness of the hills to climb and descend which, like the global economic environment, is mostly beyond our control. Too fast downhill, and the truck can lose control and crash—not a big worry anytime soon. Too slow uphill, and the truck stalls or even backslides. The truck, like the economy, has to keep moving, or the drivers and owners can't get paid, and in turn can't pay their bills.

The truck of the US economy practically stopped in the crisis of 2008. To keep it going, the government took off all the interest rate brakes, and applied full gas with spending and money supply. Over the following years we've finally gained back a little speed, but we are still going slowly. Fortunately, in the meantime the hills have been small, mostly one long gentle upgrade. But the gas pedal is all the way down, and we are still slow at best.

What if the road suddenly steepens, say by a financial crisis in Europe or China, or even in the US? Neither the US government nor the other major economies have more gas to apply or brakes to remove, and there are no other standard policy tools available to increase speed in the current economic conditions.

Why can't we go faster? Because our engine is not working as it could, it needs tuning and maintenance. All the power is coming from only a few cylinders: the large corporations that are squeezing maximum power out of fewer employees. Other cylinders are working weakly—the service and small-business economy. And we are carrying a heavy load of unused parts—unemployed or underemployed workers with low wages. As a result, the engine has to work harder to pull the extra weight. Left as it is, not tuned or maintained, our truck's speed and power will be more and more limited.

At the root of this are three main challenges: productivity growth, technology change, and workforce skill. While each of these threatens to get worse in the coming decade if they are not addressed on a large scale, they are also major opportunities to grow broad-based prosperity—if we can harness them effectively.

The first challenge is productivity growth, the measure of how much each worker produces on average—it is the challenge of increasing the power output of each pound of our engine. We grow productivity by using new technology and business practices to be more efficient, and we need it to grow consistently, so companies have profits to invest in expansion. If efficiency doesn't increase, jobs and wages don't grow, consumers have no more to spend, and the economy remains sluggish. Productivity has barely increased since the 2008 crash, because with current technology and business practices, there is little additional room for improvement—we are as efficient as we can be with computers and cell phones. We need fundamentally new technologies to increase the power of the engine.[55]

So the second challenge is technology change. Paradoxically, the challenge is not that we don't have the new technologies, but that we *do*. In the 2010s, industry started to employ the Internet of Things, the IoT, combining sensors and machines through computers to create smart systems that need less human supervision. Examples are self-driving vehicles and factory robots that can do more and more of the work of their human counterparts.

Despite the long-term advantages for business productivity, harnessing the new technologies to increase speed is proving highly disruptive. Using them is like supplying the economic truck with higher-grade fuel: it has the potential to produce much more power and speed than our old lower-grade fuel, but our engine needs high-tech fuel injectors to burn it. Yet we can't afford to stop the truck for a full-scale overhaul, so it must be done on the fly while maintaining our speed—much easier said than done.[56]

And this is the nature of the third challenge, workforce skill—what we need in order to use our high-tech fuel. Millions of workers lost jobs in the financial crisis of 2008-2009, and the slowest to return have been unskilled and semi-skilled jobs.[57] Now new technology is automating additional mundane tasks like repetitive factory and warehouse work, and soon truck and taxi driving. This removes additional semi-skilled jobs, yet requires more highly-skilled jobs to build and maintain the new systems—skills the newly-unemployed don't yet have.[58]

The workers are like older mechanical carburetors; they work with the old fuel, but with the new fuel they need to be remodeled as computerized fuel injectors. But the changeover is slow and difficult, and unless and until they can access the new types of jobs, the semi-skilled or unskilled workers will continue to require expensive unemployment support and social services. And they will also—understandably—agitate against the system that seemed to create their economic insecurity, or reject it altogether. The innovation economy is ready for a broad-based expansion, but the workers can't access the economy without the new skills. And if they can't access the economy, they become a drag on it. Getting access for the workers is the key.

The point, from a fundamental economic perspective, is that we can't continue as we have been and either expect a better result, or expect to respond effectively to a new economic crisis. If we continue as we have, the economy will only move slowly at best. If we hit a big hill, we could stop, or worse. And if we stay in our political deadlock, we will certainly continue as we are. We have to not only end our deadlock, but also take a new approach in policy to build speed into our economy.

The Path to Full Economic Access. To build speed into the economy we need to invest in full economic access for everyone who wants it. It is not difficult; we only need the will to make it happen. At the most fundamental level, investing in access means providing the working class and unemployed with the training and education for the innovation economy, and matching them with broader opportunities within it. Forty-five million Americans transitioning from underemployment and government assistance to productivity and prosperity is not only a protection against economic shocks, but an imperative of our principles and ideals. And it is also our biggest opportunity to build prosperity and power on the national level, because it will drive major economic expansion. The dual lynchpins to make it happen are revitalized technical training and expanded research and development.

Technical Training. To provide the working class with tools to join the innovation economy, the nation needs easier access to technical training than is currently available. But just as important, the working class also needs the family support, job placement, and relocation that allows them to effectively transition through the training to the new jobs for which they become qualified. Some might argue that providing technical training and other reemployment services is nothing new, that the government has done it for decades, with the mediocre results we see today. Yet, with a few limited exceptions, these results are due to built-in limitations of time and scope in the current system, both of which can be overcome if we have the will.

The time limitation is that even in cases where financial aid covers the full cost of a worker's new training, the time spent training is time not working to cover living expenses. Simply put, it is the rare individual who can work enough hours to support a family at a low paying job while simultaneously attending a training program for long enough to get a truly better job—let alone a technical job in the innovation economy. Unemployment benefits can help, but they are only for those who recently had a job but were laid off, and they only last a limited time. There are no benefits paid for the long-term unemployed, the chronically unskilled, or those who want to leave a poor job to retrain for a better one.

And this is the other limitation of the current system—scope. The very fact that millions of workers and families are in long-term economic struggle even when unemployment is at historic lows is the clearest evidence that existing job training systems and investments are unequal to our national economic needs and our mandate to expand power. Moving into the 2020s, when our challenge and our opportunity is not just to keep up with economic and industry needs, but to retool millions of workers to harness new technology, it is starkly apparent that we need new approaches. And we especially need approaches that not only allow workers to retrain for, find, and move to new jobs, but that provide for their families in the meantime.

We can do this quickly and comprehensively, if we are unified and motivated, because we already have proven tools at hand. As it happens, the federal government does have one small retraining program that addresses workers' needs fully, and a basic approach to retooling the workforce could be to simply expand and upgrade this program. It is called Trade Adjustment Assistance, or TAA, and it is designed to retrain workers who've lost jobs due to global trade factors such as job outsourcing to, or low-cost imports from, other countries. For these workers covered under

TAA, benefits are comprehensive: workers attend fully-paid retraining while collecting unemployment payments to cover living expenses, and they also get job placement and relocation benefits.

These benefits do have a cost to taxpayers, but it is not overwhelming: TAA costs about $13,000 per worker,[59] plus state unemployment benefits for up to two years while training, which costs another $18,000 per year based on national averages.[60] While training programs in general have had mixed results in recent decades, the key success factors are now better known, most importantly whether the training is "job-driven". In such training programs, local or regional employers have a hand in determining what skills are trained and how. This ensures that the employers get the right new employees for their needs, which in turn results in higher wages and more employment stability than other comparison groups.[61]

But despite these benefits, the TAA program is small and limited: laid-off workers only qualify when both the company and the government certify that trade was the culprit, adding up to only between 45,000 and 80,000 workers per year since 2013.[62] This is a tiny group against the over 13 million unemployed and underemployed in the US, but if expanded, the TAA structure could certainly be a workable basic approach to accomplish broad-scale comprehensive retraining.‡

Or we could take an even more advanced approach. For example, we could establish centralized national job training similar to the military school system, which is an excellent template for

---

‡ As of January 2019, the US Bureau of Labor Statistics counted 6.5 million temporarily unemployed workers, 1.3 million long-term unemployed workers who continued to search, 5.1 million part-time workers who sought full time work, and 0.4 million workers who had given up searching.[63]

how to efficiently train technical skills on a nationwide basis. We as a nation know how to do it, it is highly effective, and we can expand it to the civilian economy.

Consider: the military constantly takes new trainees and mid-career professionals alike, and relocates them to centralized facilities with large technical schools. It houses and pays them all the while. When they graduate, trainees are sent to their next jobs, with a commitment to stay in the job for a certain time. This works all throughout a service member's career, which usually involves three or four half- or full-year schools, along with several shorter two- or three-week courses for specialized skills over a twenty-year career. And when they are in school, the students can focus on training, because the rest of their lives are stable, with housing, schools for children, and steady income. It is a highly functioning system, producing the world's best educated military, and one which has high loyalty to the system that produced it. We can do this for civilian workers needing retraining and relocation as well, and instead of being a net cost to taxpayers like the military is, such a system would easily pay for itself through higher economic growth and lower welfare costs.

It would not even be complicated to establish, likely involving two tiers of technical schools, state and federal. The state level could train and match the unemployed with the open jobs in the same state, and the federal level could manage the overflow—matching excess trainees in one state with excess job openings in other states. Ideal locations for training would be mothballed military bases, which already have the infrastructure and facilities for not only training, but for housing, schools, shopping, medical care, and recreation that trainees' families would need while there.

Once a training system is up and running, it would be straightforward for the workers to access. They would start by getting online, either themselves or through a counselor, with first priority to the unemployed and the underemployed. They would select from training opportunities based on subject, geography, and pay, and be assigned a training class in the state or federal system. If the training and final job site is far enough away, the trainees and their families would be moved at no cost to them and housed temporarily at or near the school.

Whether or not they move, workers would receive a salary during training to support their families, so the workers can focus on the required training. Either before the training starts, or as it progresses, the workers would interview for and be matched with specific jobs. After graduation, they would be relocated if needed to the job at no cost to them. They would be committed to stay in their jobs, or with their employers, for a certain time based on the duration and extent of training. After the obligation is done, they would be able to move to other employers. They could continue to use the job matching services at any time, and could apply for additional retraining if the jobs in their new field are ever overfilled with workers.

While there would certainly be an initial investment to create such facilities and programs, it would not be extreme, and it would quickly become self-sustaining. The primary funding in the first few years could be drawn against the later savings in unneeded unemployment and welfare programs, and could be further subsidized by a fee from the leading companies obtaining workers through the programs.

More specifically, if we take the costs of comprehensive retraining for each worker to be about the same as a high-end TAA benefit—about $40,000 per year, all costs included—then two figures stand out regarding the economic feasibility of such an investment. The first is the annual spending on the Iraq and Afghanistan wars: over $100 billion per year.[64] That figure is relevant because we know that we as a nation can make that level of investment when we need to. If spent on retraining it could re-tool 2.5 million workers per year—twenty-five million in ten years.

The second figure is annual spending on cash and cash-like welfare payments—over $200 billion per year. This is relevant because it shows that a comprehensive retraining program would only need to reduce welfare spending by half to cover an annual investment of $100 billion. And it is certainly possible to envision even greater savings, along with increased productivity, wages, and economic power, because each re-trained worker repays a training investment in two ways: directly by becoming a taxpayer instead of an unemployment recipient, and indirectly by strengthening a business. So for the same amount the nation has spent for military operations with little economic return (aside from paying defense contractors), we can train millions more of the workers we need to grow the innovation economy.[§]

Consider how well this would work to transition millions of old-economy workers into new well-paying and stable innovation careers. Automated vehicles will soon replace truck and taxi driving, but the vehicles need to be built, controlled, and maintained by skilled technicians. Cheap natural gas and subsidized renewable

---

§ Cash and cash-like welfare includes the Earned Income Tax Credit ($55 billion), Child Tax Credit ($28 billion), Supplemental Security Income ($49 billion), Temporary Assistance to Needy Families ($18 billion), Housing Vouchers ($39 billion), and Supplemental Nutrition Assistance Program (previously Food Stamps; $79 billion).[65]

energy sources are reducing the demand for coal miners, but that means that the wind, solar and other energy technologies need skilled technicians to build, install, and maintain them. And the same is true for the manufacturing robots that are replacing the more mundane, repetitive, and lowest-paying factory jobs.

Not only are high tech, skilled jobs available today, they are even in danger of going unfilled for extended periods, slowing the economy. In 2016, a broad industry report indicated that among the job types at the greatest risk of running short of workers were plant and system operators, machinists, electricians, physical therapists, and other healthcare workers;[66] the jobs most often cited as desirable for the working class. The same year, the Manufacturing Institute, a research arm of the National Association of Manufacturers, reported that skilled manufacturing jobs—again, desirable—were getting so hard to fill that they would inhibit national manufacturing output and economic growth.[67] The US innovation economy, the strongest in the world, has high-paying, high-skill jobs. We need to get workers the skills they need, and get them matched to the jobs, to allow the economy to grow faster.

Expanded Research and Development. But even while we match workers with jobs in the immediate future, we need to ensure there will be a continued flow of high quality jobs in the coming decades as well. To do this, the innovation economy needs more research and development. And more R&D requires two things: expanded support for research universities, to ensure a continued flow of scientific discoveries; and expanded support for technology startups, to commercialize the discoveries.

Support for research universities has several benefits. First, universities create new researchers and new managers alike, which allow industry to do its own research. Second, university research labs provide excellent jobs for technicians and staff. Third, when support for universities includes tuition assistance, grants, or low-cost loans for working class students, it increases their long-term social mobility.

But, finally, and most fundamentally, supporting university research leads to new technologies, which fuel the type of industries and jobs that provide the US a competitive edge. University research has been the foundation of our innovation economy since the mid-20th century, providing the science that allows the industrial labs to create breakthrough products. Computers and wireless technology, solar and nuclear power, cancer drugs and antibiotics, and most other aspects of modern living were inspired by or have roots in the fundamental physics, chemistry, biology, and engineering of university research.

Then once new discoveries are made in the labs, they need business expertise and infrastructure to refine and commercialize them, either by startup companies, or by existing companies that buy the rights to the discoveries from the universities. So we need not only additional support for university research, but also support for technology startups and licensing.

For startup companies to form and have a chance at success, they need low-cost access to office and lab space, and to initial scale up funding. Government can help with financing, with building the lab space, and with policies to make it easier for new companies to get basic investment and to find experienced managers to run the startups. The process of finding capable managers is often the most challenging part of establishing a startup, and there is a great need for comprehensive systems to match business people with startup opportunities, and to coach and supervise their growth.

Innovation centers that have all of these elements can be highly effective at commercializing new discoveries from nearby university labs. However, the elements are not available everywhere. Many cities and states have the office and lab space, but the management teams and financing are lacking. With modest investment—including systems to connect these hubs nationwide, training for management teams, and better access to financing—individual centers can be more productive, and encourage continued technology development and spinouts from the universities. And when innovation hubs are successful, the local economies around the hubs also grow stronger. New technology companies need workers to build out more lab and office space as companies grow, they need technicians to staff the labs and run equipment, and they need services from lawyers, accountants, and IT staff to run the businesses. All of these contribute to economic growth at the local level.

And this closes the loop. Getting workers trained and matched to the new innovation jobs gives them economic access. Having skilled workers allows technology companies to create, use, and sell the new technologies of the Internet of Things. Not only are the workers employed with better pay, but the companies get more efficient through technology, and can invest in further expansion, hiring, and increased wages. And support for university research, for tuition assistance, and for innovation centers fuels new invention and new companies, helping the expansion continue.

Yet, even by choosing to create full economic access, it won't happen overnight, and it will require an investment before there is a payoff. But the eventual payoff is obvious: people become prosperous by getting stable, high-paying jobs; and people get stable high-paying jobs if they are educated, trained, and healthy.

Broad access to opportunity is the definition of the American Dream, a major part of who we are as a nation. Being born poor in America should not dictate that anyone die poor, and all people should have access to the tools to get out of poverty and have a prosperous life if they want it and are willing to work for it.

Given the opportunity to lift themselves up through effective economic reforms, forty-five million additional prosperous and productive Americans—the number currently living below the poverty line—can drive massive economic growth and power. But it can only happen if all Americans have access to that economy through tools and support. If we broaden this access as our priority, then prosperity and economic power will grow, for everyone's benefit.

<u>Economic Access and Race Relations</u>. Additionally, creating full economic access for the working class is one of our best mechanisms for improving race relations in America in the long term. Access can alleviate the economic stress on all races that drives not only police violence and the Black Lives Matter movement, but that also drives the racial stereotyping, charged rhetoric, and even the fundamental psychology of racial prejudice on which policing issues are based. Or simply consider: would race be the issue it is today if everyone, black and white, who wanted a good-paying job over the last twenty years could get it?

Economic stress is clearly a central factor in our policing issues and Black Lives Matter. Poor areas have higher crime and more aggressive law enforcement that make police shootings more common. These shootings lead to charges of systemic racism not only in policing, but also in government and in society more generally. Groups supporting police often react angrily to such charges, further increasing tensions.

Yet economic stress has been a central factor in our racial divide long before Black Lives Matter and the first protests in Ferguson, Missouri. For centuries around the world, persistent poverty has been the basis of the stereotype that stressed groups are inherently inferior to wealthier groups by nature of their race, and are destined to lives of poverty as a natural consequence. Such stereotyping is the definition of racism—pre-judging individual character based on race.

And it is not only stress on minorities that drives race tension: economic stress on majority groups—whites, in America—is also a major factor. In particular, it feeds resentments that government elites have coddled minorities while ignoring the needs of the white working class. This sentiment was well described in the 2016 book *Strangers In Their Own Land*, and appears to have contributed significantly Donald Trump's electoral success with white voters.[68]

And underlying it all, economic stress even appears to be a key ingredient of racial prejudice at the level of fundamental psychology. Recently published research shows that when test subjects experience an increase in economic scarcity, it increases their tendency to discriminate against people with dark skin. The conclusion is that economic stress promotes racial intolerance by itself, as a biological response to competition: it is easier to see people who look different as a threat when resources are scarce.[69]

Plainly stated, for both majority and minority groups, economic stress increases racial mistrust, and rhetoric on both sides has amplified the effect. Reducing economic insecurity and the sense of competition that it causes on all sides is the most endur-ing, self-reinforcing, and non-biased effect that public action can have on race tension. Access to high-paying jobs through training provides the resources and personal dignity to stabilize families and communities against crime, drug abuse, and scapegoating other races for economic grievances. Stable communities require less aggressive policing, reducing the chances of police shootings.

Despite this opportunity, racism of some types will probably always exist, and racist attitudes certainly cannot be legislated away. Regardless, government exists to secure our liberty, protect-ing all citizens' fundamental rights. In addressing economic stress, national action for full economic access can be a major factor in alleviating race tension in America in the long term. And in doing that, it can also alleviate one of the most potent emotional drivers of the division and polarization that damages our national power.

For all of these reasons, long-term national power must come from government that not only is efficient and adaptable, but that ensures full economic access. A strong economy requires sustain-able resources, including not only raw materials and energy, but a workforce that is educated, trained, healthy, and committed. Broad access to the economy is a critical enabler, a critical sus-tainer, and therefore a critical investment for national power.

———

So far, this chapter has described the essential principles of the role of government, which also form the basis of Principled Power—that long-term power requires efficient and adaptable government ensuring economic access for all citizens. The rest of the chapter addresses the actions that we can take to implement these principles. To summarize:

- Principle: The Constitution defines the purpose of the federal government, which is the essential institution of the United States. By the Constitution, our government exists to provide union, justice, tranquility, defense, and welfare, and to secure liberty.
- Principle: The government's mandate to promote the general Welfare means managing the public good—resources and interests by which we all benefit.
- Principle: A stable, sustainable economy is the most important public good, and to provide common benefit it must be accessible by all.

To enact these principles, we need the three reforms. The first two are based on Principled Power:

- Reform 1: The political element of power enacts our shared will, and depends on *efficient and adaptable government,* to earn the consent of the governed. To do this we must reform government administration and regulatory systems to run by broad principles and accountable leadership.
- Reform 2: The economic element of power generates our national capacity, and depends on *full economic access,* to earn our broad prosperity. We as a nation must invest in the working class as our own emerging market, to create newly skilled workers, new skilled opportunities, and new systems to match them together.

The third reform, described below, is how we get started. To apply our principles, we need a new system by which to adapt.

Reform 3: National Power Requires A New Way to Make Policy

This chapter has described the role of government in power and economic policy. But to repeat from Chapter 2, fine words and fine sentiment, but how do we make it real? How do we put Principled Power to action?

To finally implement Principled Power, we need a third reform: a new mechanism for making and implementing policy. This is because national power requires efficient and *adaptable* government, and making policy is how government adapts. Five hundred thirty-five Congress people and Senators, plus the President, buffeted by partisan politics, is no longer an effective structure for planning policy—it is not adaptable. Under obstructionism and polarization, the nation has no effective decision-making.

The Constitution gives the President the power to execute the nation's laws. This includes the power to set government policy, unless a certain policy is otherwise dictated by Congress. Under our current dysfunction however, the party out of power won't allow major new policy initiatives by the party in power. And this dynamic won't change on its own. Left only to partisan politics in the way we've let our system distort, our best policy ideas are shouted down by the loudest, richest special-interest lobbyists and the lawmakers they can influence. Certainly, electoral reforms from the previous chapter will improve compromise and reduce the influence of special interests. But electoral reforms will take time, and even then, they cannot completely eliminate the dysfunctions of how we currently make policy.

And there are other reasons for a new mechanism: to provide expert focus on our most complex challenges, to modernize our old systems, and to remain competitive in the world economy.

First, policy-making needs expert focus. The world is vastly more complex now than at our founding, and individual leaders are assaulted with a nonstop torrent of information, data, and leadership demands. Managing the complexity of our national challenges can no longer be effectively accomplished by part-time Congressional committees, or by a single President covering all issues simultaneously. While government departments and agencies can assist Congress and the President with capacity and expertise, they are generally structured to execute policies, not set them. Further, while agencies aspire to work together toward so-called "total government solutions", in reality it is a constant struggle to integrate between their bureaucratic silos. A new policy-making mechanism that sits above the department and agency level can more effectively coordinate between them.

This is related to the next reason for a new mechanism, the need to modernize. Our Constitution made us the first modern republic, and the most evolved representative government. Up through the twentieth century, our national structure provided a world-leading mix of political freedom, representation, and an increasingly industrial economy that grew incomes at all levels. Government's adaptability was adequate for the times. But since the pace of change has increased in recent years, we need to build on our political freedom, representation, and economic prowess with additional mechanisms for decisions and policies. Just as individuals and businesses constantly adapt and employ new tools for better performance, so our government needs new tools as well.

Finally, we need a new policy-making mechanism to ensure we can compete internationally. We must come to recognize that while American democracy has historically prospered from our potent mix of freedom and opportunity, we are hamstrung and falling behind other world powers in our ability to adapt, and therefore to lead. Most importantly, it is our most aggressive competitors who have the biggest advantages in this area. Because China, Russia, Iran, and other non-democracies suppress internal political opposition, they are able to focus the majority of government effort on setting and executing strategies to accomplish their national goals. There is little time or energy spent on publicly debating or justifying goals or strategies.

By comparison, in both domestic affairs and international affairs, the US is demonstrably slow and indecisive. Even against the parliamentary systems of our democratic allies, we have slowed. Government administrations in parliamentary democracies are voted-in with a mandate to execute their intended policies. It can be a challenge for them to assemble a coalition government from the multiple parties prevailing in an election, but once it is in place, the government has the power to lead the nation. To maintain international leadership and respect, and to compete, the US government must regain its ability to react and respond effectively to developments in world economics and politics.

For all these reasons—to overcome dysfunction, to provide expert focus, to modernize and to compete—American government needs a new mechanism for adapting through policy. The key question is how such a mechanism should work.

Rebuild Power by National Commissions. To implement more effective policy-making, the most fundamental problems facing our nation should be addressed using bi-partisan commissions of proven leaders, including former lawmakers and governors, with a plan of action returned to Congress to be ratified. Voters should demand that recommendations and ratification be based on building long-term national power. And voters should reserve our highest national honors and respect for those displaying the patriotism and dedication to serve on the commissions in the pursuit of our national greatness.

Lessons of Simpson-Bowles. This raises a question: Haven't we already tried commissions, most memorably the Simpson-Bowles Commission and the "Super-committee", and failed miserably?

The Simpson-Bowles Commission is essential to understand in detail because it illustrates the challenges of, and a renewed opportunity for, formulating national policy in the current environment of partisan polarization and corporate influence. By far the most important lessons to be learned from Simpson-Bowles are first, that commissions are well-equipped to make viable national policies in response to difficult issues. But second, commissioners who will eventually run for re-election cannot compromise effectively in the current environment—although former officials can.

The Simpson-Bowles Commission (formally the National Commission on Fiscal Responsibility and Reform) was created by President Obama in 2010 to identify "policies to improve the fiscal situation in the medium term and to achieve fiscal sustainability over the long run." The commission consisted of 18 members, six each from the House and Senate, and six Presidential appointments. Of the lawmakers, there were equal numbers of Democrats and Republicans; the President's appointments were Democrats or independents.[70]

The commission first met in late April 2010, and released its official report on December 1 of that year. In between, the commission held numerous public and private hearings gathering input and information from top executives and other experts from organizations both inside and outside government. These included leaders of the Federal Reserve, the Office of Management and Budget, the Congressional Budget Office, the International Monetary fund, the Organization for Economic Cooperation and Development, the Committee for a Responsible Federal Budget, and the Government Accountability Office, along with a range of academic and private-sector leaders and experts.

In early November, the co-chairs released a draft proposal for consideration by the commissioners, generating a predictable mix of public support and criticism—predictably Democrats protesting spending cuts and Republicans protesting tax increases. The following month, the commission released its final plan. In outline, the plan was designed to reduce federal deficit spending by $4 trillion over ten years, reduce debt from over 60% of GDP to under 40% by 2035, and reduce federal outlays from 28 percent of GDP to match revenues at 21 percent of GDP by 2035. About two-thirds of the deficit reduction would come from spending cuts and reforms, and one third from tax increases and reforms.

To send their final recommendations to Congress for approval, the commission needed the endorsement of 14 of its 18 members, yet fell short in the end with only 11 votes, split equally between

Democrats and Republicans with one independent. With no vote in Congress, in the following weeks and months the plan simply became fuel for the intensifying budget debate that exemplified our political dysfunction and deadlock.

Since Simpson-Bowles the nation has lurched on through further infamous phases of debt reduction efforts: the so-called Super-committee, fiscal cliff, and multiple debt ceiling / government shutdown dramas. And we ended up with the budget sequester, government spending caps designed in 2012 to be political punishment against Congress for not compromising, but only punishing the nation as a whole instead.

Because in the end the Simpson-Bowles plan was not endorsed by a supermajority of even the commission itself, it is tempting to dismiss bipartisan national commissions as a failed concept, but it is a mistake to do so. Rather, Simpson-Bowles teaches us three critical lessons, the first of which is that commissions of experienced political leaders can create strategic solutions to politically-difficult national challenges in reasonable timeframes.

The second lesson is that while it is valuable to include commissioners who are experienced lawmakers and governors, they should be *former* lawmakers and governors, because currently-serving leaders are not able to sell the final compromises to their party constituents in the existing political environment.

And the third lesson is that regardless of how we assess the specific recommendations, it is hard to believe the plans of a diligent commission acting in good faith will be worse than continued deadlock. (And more so, if a commission remained standing after its final report to monitor and update its plans and recommendations over time, it is likely to be even more effective.)

Structuring National Commissions. By applying the lessons of Simpson-Bowles, we can employ a new form of bipartisan commission as the mechanism we need for creating efficient policies to expand our power.

Structuring commissions is relatively simple; half of the commissioners would be appointed by each party, for a total between fourteen and eighteen. And again, these bipartisan commissions would differ from Simpson-Bowles in one most critical respect: no commissioners can be current governors or members of Congress, so they will not need to campaign for re-election, and they must be sworn against running in the future as well. Congress would simply charge commissions to create coherent national policies in our most critical and controversial areas of government policy, and to ensure the policies provide the greatest contribution to long-term national power for a manageable national investment. This is Principled Power at work as a guide for national policy.

What types of challenges and solutions are appropriate for national commissions? Any great challenge of national importance on which we are deadlocked and politically polarized:

- Government financing and taxes
- Government efficiency and regulation
- Economic access
- Energy and the environment
- Healthcare
- Immigration

A main advantage of a system of national commissions is its

natural flexibility: commissions can be created and employed when needed, to address specific issues.

Based on Principled Power and the role of government, three commissions in particular are clearly essential to make a commission system work overall. The first two are commissions to refine and monitor the reforms described in this chapter for efficient government (Reform 1), and for full economic access (Reform 2). The third essential commission is for government finance and taxes—the unfinished work of the Simpson-Bowles Commission—because sustainable government fiscal policy is critical for national power. Additionally, the first and third commissions are also essential to manage and prioritize the impact of any other commissions' plans on government operations, or the needs for public funding, respectively.

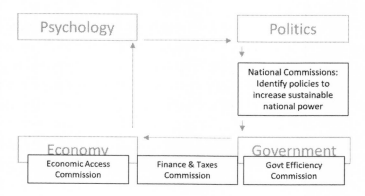

For commissions to be effective, their recommendations would need to be binding on Congress by default, once a plan is endorsed by 2/3 of its commissioners. Congress should retain the power to reject any plan by its own 2/3 vote, for which they would answer in the next election. To alter a plan, Congress should be required to win the endorsement of 2/3 of the plan's commission; otherwise, plans will be hostage to political grandstanding, delay, and deadlock. In these ways, a commission system would maintain checks and balances while creating what Francis Fukuyama recommends to fix the vetocracy: a "mechanism to promote stronger hierarchical authority within the existing system of separated powers."

Crucially, commissions including former governors and lawmakers would have the experience and perspective to take domestic political considerations into account in their deliberations, without being subject to re-election politics or the need to maintain the rhetoric of the permanent campaign themselves. With such dynamics, commissions can plan difficult trade-offs when needed, and can explain to both parties why trade-offs are needed for the nation in the long run.

Once a plan is ratified, the commission would transition to an initial implementation phase, guiding Congress and the administration in enacting additional legislation and embarking on the national plans. Following this would be a third phase for each commission, consisting of tracking the implementation, reporting publicly on progress, and recommending periodic adjustments. On a regular basis, the commission would be replaced with new members who would conduct an assessment of progress, and continue as appropriate. Finally, all commissions would have a sunset date after twenty years, when they will disband if not reinstated by Congress.

If our political debate is re-oriented towards long-term national power driven by efficient and adaptable government ensuring full access to the economy, this policy mechanism provides what our political polarization no longer allows. It provides a deliberative process that weighs all evidence and forms real, long term solutions—solutions to advance our national interests in allegiance to our first principles.

Re-orienting the debate towards power is also essential because after a commission makes its recommendations, the process reverts to the politics of Congressional and final Presidential approval. At this point, commission plans would be subject to the influence of corporations and special interests, unless Principled Power and an Electoral Reform Act have been seriously debated, if not formally endorsed and enacted by both major political parties before commissions are instituted. If they have been debated and endorsed, it is more likely that a system of commissions will have the political support to prevent special interests from derailing resulting policies and legislation, or negotiating special perks through the process. Even so, in this system corporations *benefit* in the long run through the commissions' focus on a healthy economy. Policy-making will become effective in the face of special interests and partisan politics.

Can the market best expand our national power in a given challenge, or can a government initiative do it (or a combination of the two)? What is the full range of feasible solutions to a given challenge? What is the cost in time and money of each solution, and would the result expand our broad prosperity? We need to have our best minds and our most experienced leaders assess all of the available knowledge and formulate a comprehensive American strategy in each case. This is how the Constitution was created, and how the nation can prosper for many generations to come.

In summary, our first principles mandate that we expand both the will and the capacity for national power, and government is an essential link between them, connecting politics to economics. Once politics is capable of shared will through electoral reform, government must be able to expand economic capacity, and do it efficiently. In recent decades however, excessive bureaucracy and regulation have damaged public trust in government, blocking the will and resources that government needs to expand economic capacity, further decreasing trust and our national power in a downward spiral.

<u>Do the Right Thing</u>. To restore public trust and expand power we must create bipartisan commissions of experienced leaders, charged to design and oversee national policies for expanding long-term American power. Within this system, three commissions are essential: commissions on government efficiency and regulation, on economic access, and on government finance and taxes.

An efficiency commission would be able to restore effectiveness to and trust in government by replacing volumes of detailed rules with fewer and broader principles and objectives, and holding leaders accountable for them. An access commission would be able to expand economic capacity by investing in research and in skills retraining for workers, to increase productivity by full access to the innovation economy. And a finance commission would be able to coordinate the resources government needs to make these reforms, ensuring long term fiscal sustainability that balances expansion and prosperity in the present with investment for the future.

Ultimately, such reforms realign government in its essential role to secure all citizens' rights and liberty not only by providing justice and defense, but also by managing the prime public good of a strong and sustainable national economy.

As individuals, regardless of party affiliation, we can make this happen by supporting the independent groups that advocate for these reforms, and talking about our intent to vote on reform issues. The choice is ours.

Effects of Electoral Reform and National Commissions

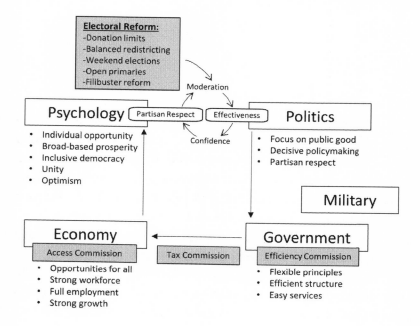

Five

Choosing Our Future

Imagine two nations, each representing what America could be at mid-century. What separates these possible futures is whether we maintain our polarized political dysfunction in the coming decades, or reform it. Both of these future nations enter the 2020's the same way, and both have vigorously debated politics, but that is where most of the similarities end.

In the first nation, we maintain today's politics for the long term, with the two main parties in a polarized equilibrium. Discontent continues to produce partisan outrage at both ends of the spectrum, but electoral battles and the permanent campaign provide an adequate pressure release, preventing unrest.

At midcentury in this nation, candidates for any office still begin each election cycle with private fundraising. With it, corporations, billionaires, and political party leadership continue to control access to primaries and thus to elected office. Winning candidates, except for the independently wealthy, are beholden to their donors, who exercise influence largely for their own benefit.

The legislature is evenly divided between the two major parties most of the time, 50-50 or nearly so. All issues great and small are politicized, and solutions are obstructed by the minority party for negotiating leverage. Both parties continue to support filibuster rules in the upper chamber, allowing any Senator to block any measure from coming to a vote. By continued obstruction, the minority can gain marginal power through voter frustration, and be able to win additional Congressional seats in the next election, allowing the process to repeat with the other party.

Society and the economy have become as polarized as politics; economic class of birth completely determines economic opportunity and political voice. Those in the corporate, professional and executive classes can provide good, sheltered lives for their families. They are able to show their kids the same path, and have the resources to educate and supervise them. Parents do this intensively, providing the requisite resume-building experiences for access to good colleges and professional jobs.

Lower on the income scale, the lives of the working class have worsened, as workers increasingly struggle to pay for education, retirement, and health. Government programs to support job training and child care, long stuck in the legislative deadlock, have dwindled. Cash-strapped workers find it almost impossible to train for emerging job opportunities. Upward mobility is limited to those with time and money to invest in education and training. Economic and social mobility for the middle class and below runs almost exclusively downward.

Both rural and urban working class areas have experienced several decades of increased drug use and growing despondency. Racial issues, hardened on party lines and deadlocked with other major issues, have intensified and periodically flash to unrest. Incarceration rates, already the world's highest in the early century, have increased further.

Municipalities, from small rural towns to large cities, provide only the most minimal services outside the wealthiest districts. Housing, infrastructure, policing, and social services have decayed over time from dwindling tax bases in most areas, while professionals and the wealthy entirely isolate themselves in well-funded enclaves. Private philanthropy partially fills the vacuum of reduced government support in poor areas, but it is haphazard and uncoordinated, and shrinks from lack of resources when it is needed most, in downturn years.

Adversarial politics at home have long prevented coherent and effective foreign policy. Other countries have turned less and less to the nation for international leadership, knowing that very few agreements or treaties made by the President will ever be ratified by the legislature.

Overall, the system is consistent and predictable. The unemployment rate appears low, although the poor work only part-time jobs out of necessity, or simply don't participate in the work force. The national economy, sustained by the profits of major corporations, oscillates between low growth and intermittent recession. For most people, daily living is marked by a feeling of uncertainty and tension, and a longstanding sense of empty national principles and greatness lost. Whatever party is in power in any given year blames the opposition for blocking its sensible plans to increase prosperity. The minority party insists that the majority party's policies are the source of the nation's problems, and that the minority party will truly increase prosperity if elected in the next vote.

———————

Now imagine the second nation. This nation has taken a different political path, instituting modest reforms of politics and government. The reforms were designed to restore the nation's ability to adapt to a changing world, and to provide better freedom and prosperity at mid-century than in the early decades of the century.

At mid-century in this nation, election cycles also begin with fundraising, as they had previously. However, donations may only be accepted from individual citizens, and are limited in size; the ceiling generally equals the going poverty-level wage, which has grown only slightly from the 2010's, when it was about $25,000. Corporations, lobbyists, and trade groups may not donate.

In this nation, super PACs and anonymous political speech in general have long been banned by law. Further, no political electioneering ads or statements are allowed from corporations or politically-oriented social welfare groups, and any ads not made directly by a candidate's campaign must identify the individual funder by name. Ads focus on their own candidate's positions and qualities; attack ads are in the minority. Most electoral finance is from small and medium donations which go directly to campaigns. A system of public-only election financing has been under consideration in recent years.

All primary elections are open to all parties and candidates, with first and second-place winners advancing to the general election. Voting districts are drawn by bipartisan commissions with mandates for political blindness. With high primary turnout, politicians address themselves to the entire electorate in primaries and general elections alike.

Election day has long since moved to the weekend. Voter turnout is always high, representing all parts of the spectrum. Voters know where candidates stand on relevant issues. Candidates are successful by consistently responding to the majority of their constituents, and the center of gravity of politics is the discussion between candidates and the electorate, instead of between candidates and wealthy donors.

Once in office, both liberal and conservative politicians' agendas overlap significantly. Politicians advance careers by collaborating and building coalitions with other government leaders to address issues and to advance the real prosperity of their constituents. The balance of party power in the legislature is less consequential than in more polarized nations. Liberals and conservatives exist in both parties, as defined by local interests, and party platforms have many commonalities in their objectives, if not always in their proposed methodologies.

Political debate has advanced beyond a deadlocked contest for party dominance, to focus instead on how to achieve a national purpose enabled by broad prosperity and full access to economic opportunity. Voters have long since agreed that a successful nation needs broad access to education, health care, jobs with a living wage, and secure retirement, which all fuel a growing and healthy economy.

The complexity of creating and managing broad economic access required difficult political choices in prior decades. National commissions of experienced government, business and social leaders analyzed the options and recommended actions that could best provide long-term increases in broad-based prosperity. None of the issues was easy to solve, but the commissions consulted top experts and were always able over time to guide the nation's deep resources towards sustainable growth in the national interest. The economic benefits of these choices were largely realized within a decade, and continued to accelerate thereafter, steadily expanding the nation's cultural, diplomatic, and military power worldwide.

The commissioners themselves became experts in the nation's most important issues, and continue to monitor the financing and implementation of sustainable national policies for each. The legislature ratifies or rejects the plans as they evolve. Legislators and commissioners alike are respected for providing vision and results in the national interest.

The nation has struck a sustainable balance of taxes and spending. Working for the long term, government was modernized in previous decades to be highly efficient, and to focus on managing vibrant markets with broad access for labor and competitors, and on managing market externalities. Government is small, easy to use, and efficient.

Realizing the economic importance of scientific discovery, national commissions years ago re-instituted major funding for universities and national labs. By midcentury, consistent investment had provided three decades of economic expansion in technical industries. At the base is a humming engine of development based on discoveries in all areas of physics, math, biology, and chemistry.

Engineers have steadily applied the discoveries to new inventions, originally in areas of energy, robotics, sensors, and personalized medicine, and later in technologies that had been completely unknown and unforeseeable at the century's beginning. The nation's universities, always known as the world's finest, have become even more central to the resurgent economy, a system other nations have worked hard to emulate.

While major corporations remain important to the economy, they have been replaced as the main drivers of prosperity by the startup technology companies. As new discoveries and inventions are made in the universities, they are commercialized by teams of entrepreneurs, investors, and new university and technical school graduates. Government has long since focused on making new companies easy to start and grow.

As they grow, companies not only directly employ managers, support staff, and researchers, but also indirectly the workers and staff for the buildings, equipment, infrastructure, and support services they need along the way. Successful startups and their employees are bought by major corporations or grow into major corporations themselves. The unsuccessful startups disband, providing experienced managers to commercialize other discoveries. Investment returns are sustainably higher than in previous decades, as technology companies making materials, devices and equipment have outpaced companies from the early century based on consumer internet applications, finance, food, and entertainment.

Relying on proximity to universities to start and grow, the technology companies and their jobs are purely domestic, becoming the heart of a sustainable prosperity that provides true economic power to the nation. This economy is adaptable: while new technologies make older ones obsolete, the nation is always at the technical forefront, and workers can retrain to keep the needed skills. The economy is also self-renewing, based on a consistent flow of discovery.

Finally, the economy is multi-leveled. At the foundation are research & development, process development, and high-technology manufacturing in different geographic areas of expertise around the country; transportation technology in some regions; communications, medicine, or others elsewhere. Resting on that foundation are construction, business services, healthcare, and consumer services everywhere. Low-skilled commodity manufacturing is still done overseas for efficiency, but higher skills and higher pay remain at home.

High-technology manufacturing hubs form and thrive in rural areas, where land and labor are less expensive. Research, development, and business service hubs predominate in revitalized urban areas, where proximity to universities, business services, and professional labor is more critical. Regardless, distinctions between urban and rural living are less pronounced than in previous generations. Steady economic growth has allowed communities in all areas to redesign residential areas around walkable neighborhoods where people have homes, jobs, and recreation in easy access. Long commutes for workers are less common, leaving more time for leisure and family.

Economic opportunity and wise investment have dramatically reduced outright poverty. Employment is high, with well-paying jobs for the revitalized working class. Job training, decent schools, and accessible healthcare provide stability for working families and communities. Affordable child care has allowed millions more women to attend technical training and then to work, sharply reducing welfare and increasing social mobility.

All workers have affordable access to functioning education, including college and technical training. Technical schools have become central to the economy, as sources of high-skilled labor and of upward mobility for the working class. The types of training available at the technical schools are based on the needs of different industries nationwide. Workers, including those in mid-career, select training based on topic, geography, and pay, and are matched to jobs as their training progresses.

More importantly, technical retraining in mid-career has had a major impact on national productivity, allowing workers to update skills, keep pace with rapid technology advances, and build lasting careers. Training costs are subsidized both by the leading companies and by public funds saved from unneeded welfare programs. Mid-career workers who enter retraining receive a stipend for family support while taking classes. Resulting high wages and high employment more than cover the costs of the retraining.

Based on this, the nation increasingly values skilled technical work as a lifestyle and livelihood, providing a sought-after combination of good pay, fulfillment, and work-life balance. At the same time, increasingly-affordable colleges and graduate schools allow more and more working class students to get the education to enter professional, business, and scientific careers, with the associated mobility. Economic stability for the working class has greatly diminished crime, incarceration rates and racial tensions.

In the media, the main national dramas are based not on partisan political deadlock, but on ending poverty domestically, on maintaining a stable economy internationally, and on assisting the peaceful transition of unstable regions abroad towards productive economies respecting international laws. The nation takes great pride in being universally accepted as the world's leader, and as the essential partner for managing world crises. By its economic and military strength, the nation provides the protection and leadership for troubled regions overseas to internally stabilize the most troubled countries among them. International markets continue to expand, providing growth opportunities worldwide for the nation's successful businesses.

None of these advances has come instantly or without debate, but the nation's political conversation accepts that properly-functioning government responding to the citizens' needs is the highest achievement of the nation's principles. The nation understands that broad prosperity is the only sustainable way to ensure the union, justice, tranquility, defense and welfare that secure the citizens' liberty in the long term.

This nation's politics are about broad prosperity and economic access, and the best leaders rise to historical prominence for good reason. The nation understands where it is and where it is going. This nation is the example of the virtue of a pluralistic society under the rule of law, where all have the opportunity to earn a decent living, or even to achieve greatness.

Both of these futures are foreseeable at midcentury. One is based on a continuation of our current path and trends, and the other is based on modest political reforms and renewed government function.

Yet there is also a third future, or category of futures, that is foreseeable. However, its possible pathways and outcomes at mid-century are more numerous and harder to predict. These are the futures in which we maintain our politics, yet our electoral cycle and the permanent campaign no longer serve as adequate pressure releases. Instead of maintaining or reforming government, we reject it in favor of another.

Such a scenario might begin in the coming decade. While the upper class and a small segment of the middle class gain an increasing share of national income and political power, mobility for most of the middle class and below runs increasingly downward. With no serious prospect of change through the stagnated political system, working class discontent boils to unrest.

Ominously, the unrest forms in different ways among different groups; the only common theme is protecting local and group interest against a national political and economic system that is increasingly unresponsive to the needs of most citizens. It is an uprising without cohesion—a melting pot that concludes that the system cannot in fact provide opportunity or freedom, or protect most people's rights through national government. In multiple ways and by multiple forces, the nation fractures.

In rural towns and counties, the white working class and chronically unemployed become so economically stressed and hopeless that they increasingly identify with anti-government extremist groups. As more people join these groups, the most militant among them mount ever-larger anti-government armed standoffs in rural towns and counties, and on federal lands. While the different groups present a confusing mix of different demands—greater local autonomy, freedom from federal taxes, more jobs—increasing numbers of the rural working class cheer the general resistance against undemocratic and self-serving national government. Protests and standoffs multiply, and frequent media images of federal agents surrounding and arresting protesters feed a narrative that the central government is remote, run by elites, and holding power by force.

At the same time, racial tensions grow. Like the anti-federal groups, yet for their own reasons, minority communities become ever more mistrustful of and frustrated with government and its inability to address their grievances, and they continue to self-organize at the local level. Police shootings, previously in decline, become more frequent, fueling mass protests by minority groups and their supporters, and inspiring reprisal attacks on police. Counter-movements for law and order intensify in many white communities, widening the divide.

As society becomes more disordered, communities across the nation turn further inward, looking to city and town councils to ensure basic services are secure, and can continue to provide a sense of normal life. In the capital, the existing two-party standoff degenerates into a multi-sided cacophony of discontent, grievance, and finger-pointing, and no substantive legislation or policy proposals can achieve the votes to move forward. Congress is completely paralyzed.

Amid this confusing array of new factions, an anti-federal party forms and gathers strength, its philosophy of minimal government appealing to the interest in local empowerment common around the nation. Combining the existing political connections of its founding factions and the groundswell of popular support, the party gains the allegiance of a plurality of state governments and congressional delegations. As its political momentum builds, the party seizes the chance to realize a longstanding dream of its founders, and openly calls for re-writing the Constitution to create a new government based on local and individual autonomy.

In the meantime, political paralysis continues. The uncertainty has slowed the national economy; layoffs are increasingly widespread and further increase dissatisfaction and tension among the working class. Many large corporations announce plans to move more operations to foreign locations as a hedge against political uncertainty. The corporations also support the authority of the federal government, increasingly putting them at political odds with the working class. Wanting to protect their own economic stability, the affluent and the professional classes also support the federal system, further hardening social divisions along lines of economic class. Overseas, international business and markets increasingly come to rely on the German, French, and Chinese governments to provide rational decision-making. The European Union, destabilized by a wave of large-country exits and a widening gap between its own rich and poor member states, disbands.

As these dynamics intensify worldwide, capital markets finally seize up completely, slowing or stopping most other business operations. The federal government, despite understanding from the lessons of 2008 what actions are necessary to prevent economic disaster, is only able to enact a weak stimulus program to restart financial activity. Anti-government factions, suspicious of federal authority and increasingly united in the interest of local empowerment, resist all stronger measures.

In a matter of months, with the crippled economy further swelling the ranks of the unemployed, political and business leaders acquiesce to anti-federal demands to rewrite the Constitution. Rumors circulate that the most radical populists in the legislature forced the deal as a condition for agreeing to the stimulus and saving the economy. A Constitutional convention is presented with a preexisting draft in which political power is newly concentrated at the local levels. The power of municipalities supersedes the power of states, which supersedes the power of a weak federal government. The draft is ratified with few alterations.*

In the decades following the new constitution, the economy struggles. Because financial markets were only partially revived, it is eventually understood that the depression is a deeper, longer version of the crisis of 2008-2009. Unemployment is high, varying between 20% and 40%. The combination of smaller markets and high uncertainty prevents business investment, and economists come to believe the conditions represent a new permanent equilibrium.

In these years, the anti-federalists, still the majority, maintain consensus that state-based economies will emerge to provide full employment. They say these new economies will be well adapted to local conditions, and provide more fairness and equity than the previous economic system. Barter economies, enabled by mobile technology, match buyers and sellers with greater efficiency than ever before. However, the benefit cannot offset the overall economic contraction and the crippled labor and credit markets.

---

* While this sequence of events is conjectural, forecasting what might follow is even more so. However, educated guesses are possible given the recent histories of sudden societal changes, including the breakups of the Soviet Union and Yugoslavia, the aftermath of the Iraq invasion, the financial crisis of 2008-2009, and the uprisings of the Arab spring. Based on them, the rest of the chapter describes a relatively mild trajectory for this type of scenario.

Overseas, large autocratic rival nations have capitalized on the nation's weakness. With their own recessions spawned by the nation's economic contraction, they each declare states of emergency and violently eliminate all political dissent to their ruling parties. With domestic political authority consolidated in each country, they are able to coordinate industrial production to fill the shortfalls of the nation's once-powerful manufacturing sector. They steal market share in some industries, and fully monopolize others. With increasing economic power, the autocracies increasingly set the terms of international affairs.

In the face of these rising foreign powers, the nation continues to morally support its military, but the military budget falls by 90% through a combination of weak federal tax authority, and reduced taxable income. While the military remains a capable homeland defense force, it lacks the logistics, fuel, and spare parts to operate outside its borders. Overseas bases are abandoned, and large portions of the air force and navy are mothballed at domestic bases.

The autocracies, no longer constrained from aggression, seize key economic resources outside their borders. In an increasingly familiar pattern, one or the other autocracy reports that a certain region is falling victim to instability or humanitarian injustice, and the autocracy occupies the region militarily, creating a special protection area in the name of stability. The occupier then remains to administer and protect the area pending handover to the UN, although the handovers never come to pass.

Every year the number of special protection areas grows in resource rich parts of Africa, Asia, and in later years in South America. Key shipping lanes in the South Pacific, South Atlantic, and Indian Oceans are secured against piracy, as the autocracies put it. Ships from every nation must pay an escort fee for protected transit.

In parallel, strong-arm business practices and political practices increase inside the nation itself, as they have in all the other democracies. Amid instability and uncertainty, political leaders offering stability and order rise quickly to power. Without significant tax revenues, police and the courts can offer only limited public law enforcement. In response, private firms fill the gap with locally based security services charging ever higher fees. In time, security executives increasingly hold formal political power, converting profits and security power to elected office. Businesses pay high premiums to ensure smooth operations and deliveries of products. Local governments rarely prosecute allegations of intimidation or attacks on companies that do not pay for private security. Eventually most companies acquire private protection.

While disturbing, such practices prove mild compared with the turbulence in most other nations. With the ongoing global depression, social and economic tensions worldwide accelerate to violence in most countries until suppressed by their governments. Military dictatorships have dominated for several years among the poor nations. Regions without a single dominant group have devolved to persistent civil war.

At home, the nation's political leaders offer the vision of a future with a stable economy and increased employment. Confronted with the persistent economic weakness under the new constitution, politicians argue that once there is a recovery, whenever it may come, the economy will be fairer, more balanced, and more just. Asked if it will be worth it, they say there is no point wondering, because there is no going back anyway.

———

While future paths such as this one are more radical by definition, they are certainly plausible. They do not require all, or even a majority of the population to get underway. There is certainly a significant proportion of American citizens who, while they may not have a commonly-agreed alternative government, are sufficiently disillusioned with our current dysfunction to consider radical alternatives. And among this proportion, some groups are viscerally angry to the point of being enraged. Rage, stoked by political opportunists or heating on its own to the boiling point, can surge rapidly out of control to violence and chaos, even in America—as our periodic urban riots have repeatedly shown.

So rejecting or attempting to reject the government is indeed a possible future. How intolerable would life have to be to bring this about? Would we be rejecting and replacing our government as a positive choice, or as a miserable last resort when all else has failed? Or even when, as Niall Ferguson warns, the society suddenly collapses? Given how radical the changes would be, is it even possible to imagine a scenario that wouldn't involve serious violence (unless it is with serious curtailment of civil liberty)? This is where this other future takes us, with more questions than answers, and none of them particularly attractive.

What nation do you want for your children and their families? What nation do you want to see around you in your last years? Which nation should win?

Conclusion

If our current political dysfunction has any benefit, it is to shine a light on the importance of our national first principles of democracy, and on the path we are choosing when we neglect them and indulge partisanship first. It is time in America for individual citizens to decide whether we continue toward a parody of our democracy's original promise, or regain the path toward our national aspirations. We aspire to be a model republic—an example to the world of the virtue of a pluralistic society under the rule of law where all citizens have the opportunity to achieve according to their talents. To regain the path, we need to first acknowledge the current realities of our politics and our governmental function:

Our political form is sound in its basic design, yet has been distorted over time and by different interests. In recent years this has transferred excessive political power to corporations and to extremely wealthy individuals.

First, electoral financing is distorted so that most politicians are beholden to a small number of wealthy donors and companies, both of whose interests now hold sway. Second, voting practices are distorted to favor incumbent candidates and uncompromising extremism, rewarding legislative deadlock. And third, this extremism and deadlock block government in its roles of justice, defense, and the public good, crippling the public's trust and eroding our national power.

The winners in this deadlocked system are small in number, yet wield inordinate political power. They have interconnected incentives to maintain our deadlock in the long term. The winners include:

Wealthy donors, corporations, and lobby groups, which gain unparalleled political influence with elected officials by funding campaigns, and can enact legislation that benefits their interests as the price of ending stalemates.

Political consultants, super-PAC fundraisers, and professional campaigners who grow in number and salary as donations and media campaigns expand.

Media companies, which benefit directly by selling ever more advertising time to the campaigns, and indirectly by maintaining the drama of partisan rivalry, for higher news and pundit ratings. Conflict sells.

Finally, the executives and staff of the major political parties, and their derivative PACs and issue groups, who gain in stature and influence as first among equals of their parties' factions.

The losers of this system are the vast majority of American citizens, and the legacy of American democracy itself. The more power the nation loses by deadlock and mistrust of government, the more power donors, corporations, and lobby groups gain domestically, and autocratic rivals gain overseas.

Given these realities, it is time we commit both individually and collectively to rebuild our national power. And we must do it efficiently and responsibly, for all Americans and not only a few at the top. To do this we need the shared will of Principled Power: adaptable and efficient government ensuring full economic access, to focus policy on national power for the greatest good, to secure our liberty.

S. J. Reynolds

<u>Our Collective Actions</u>. Regardless of our party affiliations, we all as American citizens must restore the responsiveness and adaptability of American government as intended by the Constitution, in accordance with our national first principles.

1. We must reform our electoral financing in accordance with our principles of accountable speech. Our most important collective action is to support *an amendment or equivalent Constitutional authority* for Congress to regulate political speech by corporations and associations, including super PACs. Once this is done, we must push Congress for an *Electoral Reform Act*, eliminating super PACs and campaign contributions by lobbyists and government contractors, and tightening and enforcing contribution limits and rules on disclosure.

2. We must reform other electoral practices in accordance with our principles of fair voting. An Electoral Reform Act must require balanced and party-blind redistricting, weekend elections, and open primaries, and it must also reform Senate filibuster practices.

3. We must create bipartisan commissions of proven leaders to design and oversee national policies for expanding long-term American power amid the reality of modern party politics. Among these, commissions on government finance and taxes, government efficiency and regulation, and economic access are most essential to put our national ideals to action in support of our national power.

136

<u>Our Individual Actions</u>. There can be no collective action without individual action, and while the reforms we need are broad, and the path will be long, the first steps are simple. To begin real change, we must write our representatives and candidates to support reforms, we must join and support the independent groups that advocate for these reforms, and we must talk openly about our intent to vote on reform issues above all others. Without reform, all of our other political efforts merely prolong and intensify our dysfunction. And among the reform issues, the most urgent is demanding that our representatives vote to eliminate super PACs and other sources of anonymous paid political speech by corporations and the wealthy.

If we can talk boldly about why we need national power over the long term as our first concern, how we grow it, and how we use it, we can return our politics and our government to their proper function.

We will owe the future greatness of our country to those who will lead by this, knowing that in the end, history will judge America by our dedication to our national principles. These are our first principles of freedom and opportunity. They guide a nation in adapting to all ages, through our Constitutional design by, for, and of the people, for ourselves and our posterity, who are blessed and proud to call ourselves Americans.

Appendix

Sample Letter to a Member of Congress

Dear Representative _____ ,

I am writing to voice my support for a non-partisan Electoral Reform Act to help reverse our destructive political polarization. This polarization has deadlocked our politics and our government, and because it prevents us from solving any of our other issues, it is pushing the country to decline.

We might not agree on every issue, but regardless of party we all have a stake in ensuring our political system is based on the equal vote of citizens in fair and open elections, and not on the influence of paid special interests. However, our system is now distorted to favor these special interests, and to maintain our partisan deadlock. To correct this, we need an Electoral Reform Act that will: eliminate super PACs and other tools of anonymous political speech; end the Senate filibuster as a tool of obstruction; and establish party-blind redistricting, weekend elections, and open primaries. Such a Reform Act can ensure that officials represent the interests of all their local voters, above the interests of paid partisan groups with narrow agendas.

I believe we can end the polarization that is tearing the country apart, and restore the democracy America is meant to be. That is why I support these reforms, and why I want my representatives to do the same. Thank you for your consideration, and for your service to the country.

Sincerely,

Reform Groups

The remainder of the appendix provides a list of reform groups that advocate for and promote the types of reforms described in *Principled Power.* Certain groups focus on certain reforms: electoral laws and finance, policy-making, and/or government efficiency.

Bipartisan reforms in all these areas are essential to building America's national power in the 21st century. As individuals, regardless of party affiliation, we can make this happen by supporting the independent groups that advocate for these reforms, and talking about our intent to vote on reform issues. The choice is ours.

For comprehensive reform (including electoral laws and finance, policy-making, and government efficiency)

Principled Power
Principled-power.org
This organization was founded by the author to promote the reforms described in *Principled Power*.

For electoral finance reform (alphabetical order):

Center for Responsive Politics
Opensecrets.org
From the 2019 website: "Our Vision and Mission: Inform, Empower & Advocate. Nonpartisan, independent and nonprofit, the Center for Responsive Politics is the nation's premier research group tracking money in U.S. politics and its effect on elections and public policy. Our vision is for Americans, empowered by

access to clear and unbiased information about money's role in politics and policy, to use that knowledge to strengthen our democracy. Our mission is to produce and disseminate peerless data and analysis on money in politics to inform and engage Americans, champion transparency, and expose disproportionate or undue influence on public policy."

Issue One
Issueone.org
From the 2019 website: "Issue One is the leading cross-partisan political reform group in Washington. We unite Republicans, Democrats, and independents in the movement to fix our broken political system.

Fixing America's Political System So Our Democracy Works for Us

We live in turbulent times, and Americans are yearning for change. Issue One is uniquely positioned to seize this historic opportunity and win bold, national political reforms—to strengthen ethics laws, reduce the influence of big money on politics, modernize elections and end the pay-to-play culture in Washington. We believe American Democracy is the best way to solve problems, and that fixing the system is the first step towards tackling the most critical issues facing our nation."

Mayday PAC
Mayday.us
From the 2019 website: "American citizens have had enough of big money special interests controlling our government. Members of Congress spend 70% of their time cozying up to the

well-connected few who fund their campaigns. Meanwhile, the majority of Americans get taxation without real representation.

America is no longer a government of, by, and for the people. Our Founders wanted a "representative democracy" that is "dependent on the People alone," and "not the rich, more than the poor." Our leaders are not addressing our nation's most pressing issues, favoring the interests of the well-connected few. ...

We're focusing our efforts on grassroots change—where the real power is. When the people lead, the leaders follow.

The movement to end big money politics has yet to fully leverage its power at the ballot box in an organized fashion. Other causes have successfully elected champions to advance their policies, city by city, state by state, building power and shifting policy. We should do the same. ...

To catalyze real reform sweeping the nation, we need to pass it in more cities and states to show that change is possible. Passing reform in a city in your state moves political will in your state closer to reform. Passing reform in your state moves the country closer to reform."

No Labels
Nolabels.org

From the 2019 website: "The far right and far left are holding America hostage—becoming ever more strident, uncompromising and making governance impossible. They are small in number but drive the national agenda because they are organized, because they vote, contribute to and volunteer for campaigns. In short, they show up, while the vast political center has remained on the sidelines.

No Labels is a movement for the tens of millions of Americans

141

who are fed up with the dysfunction and will no longer put up with a government that does not represent the interests of most Americans."

For government efficiency reform

Common Good

Commongood.org

From the 2019 website: "Common Good is a nonpartisan reform coalition with one basic goal—to restore the freedom of officials and citizens to use common sense.

We propose practical, bold ideas to simplify bureaucratic structures so that Americans can roll up their sleeves and get things done.

Common Good's philosophy is based on a simple but powerful idea: People, not rules, make things happen. By preventing us from using our judgment on the spot, modern bureaucracy causes failure and frustration.

Individual responsibility, not mindless compliance, must be the foundation for government just as it is in all other aspects of social life. Overhauling government to liberate human responsibility will eliminate waste in government and unleash productive activity throughout society. Just one Common Good reform—a three page statute to cut red tape in infrastructure permitting—could stimulate a million new jobs.

Our first challenge is to build support for overhaul. To do this, Common Good publishes white papers and hosts forums highlighting needless costs and paralysis, and organizes coalitions

142

behind reform proposals. Polls show that huge, bipartisan majorities of America's voters support this change in direction."

For bipartisan policy-making

Bipartisan Policy Center
Bipartisanpolicy.org
From the 2019 website: "The Bipartisan Policy Center is a nonprofit organization that combines the best ideas from both parties to promote health, security, and opportunity for all Americans. BPC drives principled and politically viable policy solutions through the power of rigorous analysis, painstaking negotiation, and aggressive advocacy.

As a Washington, D.C.-based think tank that actively promotes bipartisanship, BPC works to address the key challenges facing the nation. Our policy solutions are the product of informed deliberations by former elected and appointed officials, business and labor leaders, and academics and advocates who represent both ends of the political spectrum. We are currently focused on health, energy, national security, the economy, financial regulatory reform, housing, immigration, infrastructure, and governance."

Notes

1. Smith, M. (2016, December 16) Satisfaction With US Direction Steady but Historically Low, *Gallup.com*, http:// www.gallup.com/poll/199679/satisfaction-direction-steady-historically-low.aspx. Retrieved Jan. 15, 2017; Pew Research Center (2017, December 14) Public Trust in Government: 1958-2017, *People-press.org*, http://www.people-press. org/2017/12/14/public-trust-in-government-1958-2017/. Retrieved Feb. 19, 2018; Wall Street Journal / NBC News, polls taken Aug. 3, 2014 (76%) and Nov. 17, 2014 (56%), *WSJ.com*, http://graphics.wsj.com/wsjnbcpoll/. Retrieved from Mar. 31, 2016.

2. Colby, E. and Lettow, P. (2014, July 4) Have We Hit Peak America? The Sources of National Power and the Path to US Renaissance. *Foreign Policy*, http://foreignpolicy. com/2014/07/03/have-we-hit-peak-america/

3. Pew Research Center (2018, January 11) Three decades of congressional productivity, 1987-2017, *Pewresearch.org*, http://www.pewresearch.org/fact-tank/2018/01/11/despite-gop-control-of-congress-and-white-house-lawmaking-lagged-in-2017/ft_18-01-09_congressproductivity/. Retrieved Mar. 3, 2018; GovTrack, Statistics and Historical Comparison: Bills by final status; *Govtrack.us*, https://www. govtrack.us/congress/bills/statistics. Retrieved Aug. 18, 2018.

4. Bureau of Labor Statistics, as cited in Cohen, P. (2016, July 8) Jobs Roar Back with Gain of 287,000 in June, Easing Worry, *The New York Times*, http://www.nytimes.com/2016/07/09/business/economy/jobs-report-unemployment-wages.html. Pew Research Center (2018, August 7) For most U.S. workers, real wages have barely budged in decades, *Pewresearch. org*, http://www.pewresearch.org/fact-tank/2018/08/07/for-most-us-workers-real-wages-have-barely-budged-for-decades/.

5. Friedman T. (2014, July 15) Order vs. Disorder, Part 2, *The New York Times*, http://www.nytimes.com/2014/07/16/opinion/thomas-friedman-israeli-palestinian-conflict-order-disorder.html

6. Bremmer, Ian, *Every Nation for Itself: Winners and Losers in a G-Zero World*, Penguin Books, New York, 2012.

7. Zakaria, Fareed, *The Post-American World*, W. W. Norton & Company, New York, 2008.

8. Zakaria, p. 234

9. Zakaria, p. 237

10. Ferguson, Niall, *Civilization: The West and the Rest*, The Penguin Press, New York, 2011.

11. Ferguson, p. 324

12. Fukuyama, Francis, *Political Order and Political Decay: From the Industrial Revolution to the Globalization of Democracy*, Farrar, Straus & Giroux, New York, 2014.

13. Fukuyama, F. (1989 Summer) The End of History?, *The National Interest*, pp. 3–18.

14. Fukuyama 2014, p. 466

15. Fukuyama, p. 486

16. Luce, Edward, *The Retreat of Western Liberalism*, Atlantic Monthly Press, New York, 2017.

17. Luce, p. 73-74

18. Brill, Steven, *Tailspin: The People and Forces Behind America's Fifty-Year Fall—and Those Fighting to Reverse It*, Alfred A. Knopf, New York, 2018.

19. Brill, p. 6

20. Luce, p. 98-99

21. Ibid.

22. Fukuyama, Francis, *Identity: The Demand for Dignity and the Politics of Resentment*, Farrar, Straus and Giroux, New York, 2018.

23. Fukuyama 2018, p. 115

24. Fukuyama 2014, p. 504

25. Luce, p. 203-4

26. Brill, p. 335-341

27. Fukuyama 2018, ch. 14

28. Dionne, E. J.; Ornstein, Norman; and Mann, Thomas; *One Nation After Trump: A Guide for the Perplexed, the Disillusioned, the Desperate, and the Not-Yet Deported*, St. Martin's Press, New York, 2017, p. 73, referencing work by the political scientist David Mayhew: "divided government during the decades following World War II produced significant legislative achievements—and arguably did so as or more often than when a single party held all the reins of power."

29. Gutman, Amy, and Thompson, Dennis, *The Spirit of Compromise: Why Governing Demands It and Campaigning Undermines It*, Princeton University Press, Princeton, 2012.

30. Levitsky, Steven, and Ziblatt, Daniel, *How Democracies Die*, Crown, New York, 2018.

31. State legislature control of redistricting: from "All About Redistricting" by Loyola Law School Professor Justin Levitt,

at http://redistricting.lls.edu/ as quoted in Daley, David, *Ratf**ed: The True Story Behind the Secret Plan to Steal America's Democracy*, Liveright Publishing, 2016, p.2. 2018 update from http://redistricting.lls.edu/who-fed10.php. Retrieved Aug. 8, 2018.

32. Cost of Election, *OpenSecrets.org*, https://www.opensecrets. org/overview/cost.php?display=T&infl=Y, and Total Outside Spending by Election Cycle, Excluding Party Committees, *OpenSecrets.org*, https://www.opensecrets.org/ outsidespending/cycle_tots.php?cycle=2018&view=A&chart =N#summ , retrieved Nov. 16, 2018.

33. Herbert A. Simon, 1971, as referenced in: How the World Was Trolled (Briefing: Social Media and Politics) (2017, November 4), *The Economist*.

34. How the World Was Trolled (Briefing: Social Media and Politics) (2017, November 4), *The Economist*.

35. Russian disinformation distorts American and European democracy (Briefing) (2018, February 22), *The Economist*.

36. Sunstein, Cass, (2015) Partyism. *University of Chicago Legal Forum*, Vol. 2015, Article 2. Available at: http:// chicagounbound.uchicago.edu/uclf/vol2015/iss1/2.

37. First Principle, *Wikipedia.org*, https://en.wikipedia.org/wiki/ First_principle. Retrieved Apr. 10, 2016.

38. Jefferson, Thomas, The Declaration of Independence, (July 4, 1776). Transcript at http://www.archives.gov/exhibits/charters/declaration_transcript.html. Retrieved Aug. 31, 2015.

39. Jefferson

40. Jefferson

41. Multiple authors, The Constitution of the United States, (September 17, 1787), Transcript at http://www.archives.gov/exhibits/charters/constitution_transcript.html. Retrieved Aug. 31, 2015 (bullet point symbols added to original text).

42. Amar, Akhil Reed, *America's Constitution: A Biography*, Random House, New York, 2005, Chapter 1

43. Amar, Akhil Reed (2206) *America's Constitution* and the Yale School of Constitutional Interpretation, *The Yale Law Journal*, Vol. 115, p. 2010-2011, quoting: Koh, Harold Hongju, *The National Security Constitution: Sharing Power After the Iran-Contra Affair*, Yale University Press, New Haven, 1990, p. 74-77

44. Machiavelli, Niccolo, *The Prince*, in Beatty, John, and Johnson, Oliver (eds.), *Heritage of Western Civilization, 6th Ed.*, Prentice-Hall, Englewood Cliffs, 1987, p.385; and Hobbes, Thomas, *Leviathan*, Bobbs-Merrill, Indianapolis, 1958, p.86

45. Nye, Joseph, *Bound to Lead: The Changing Nature of American Power*, Basic Books, New York, 1990; Morganthau, Hans, *Politics Among Nations: The Struggle for Power and Peace*, 4th ed., Knopf, New York, 1968; Spanier, John and Wendzel, Robert, *Games Nations Play*, 9th ed., CQ Press, Washington DC, 1996; Couloumbis, Theodore and Wolfe, James, *Introduction to International Relations: Power and Justice*, 2nd ed., Prentice Hall, Englewood Cliffs, NJ, 1982; Nye, Joseph, *The Future of Power*, Public Affairs, New York, 2011

46. Definitions: *power*, *national power*, and *economy*, Merriam-Webster.com, http://www.merriam-webster.com/dictionary. Retrieved Jul. 12, 2016.

47. A. F. K. Organski, *World Politics*, 2d ed., New York: Knopf, 1968, p. 104

48. Jablonsky, D. (1997, Spring). National Power. *Parameters*, p. 34-54

49. Nye, *Bound to Lead*

50. Nye, *The Future of Power*, p. 25-49

51. Schmitt, M. (2012, January 22). Within Limits (Review). *The New York Times Book Review*. p. 16

52. Douthat, R. (2018, January 14). Is there Life After Liberalism? (Opinion). *The New York Times Review*, p. 9

53. Mann, Thomas, and Ornstein, Norman, *It's Even Worse Than It Looks: How the American Constitutional System Collided with the New Politics of Extremism.* Basic Books, New York, 2012.

54. Dugan, A. (2018, February 28) U.S. Satisfaction With the Government Remains Low, *Gallup.com*, https://news.gallup.com/poll/228281/satisfaction-government-remains-low.aspx. Retrieved Sept. 16, 2018.

55. Obama, B. (2016, October 8). The Way Ahead. *The Economist* http://www.economist.com/news/briefing/21708216-americas-president-writes-us-about-four-crucial-areas-unfinished-business-economic

56. Moore, S. (2015, March 31). The Great Worker Shortage. *Forbes.* Retrieved from Forbes.com. http://www.forbes.com/sites/stevemoore/2015/03/31/not-hard-at-work-hardly-working/#4d7ffc13cb78

57. Lowrey, A., (2014, April 27). Recovery Has Created Far More Low-Wage Jobs Than Better-Paid Ones, *The New York Times.* Retrieved from NYTimes.com https://www.nytimes.com/2014/04/28/business/economy/recovery-has-created-far-more-low-wage-jobs-than-better-paid-ones.html?_r=0

58. Carrick, G. and McNelly, J. (2015, April 3). *The Skills Gap in U.S. Manufacturing: 2015 and Beyond.* p.v2 Retrieved from The Manufacturing Institute, http://www.themanufacturinginstitute.org/~/media/827DBC76533942679A15EF7067A704CD.ashx

59. US Department of Labor, *Trade Adjustment Assistance for Workers Program: Fiscal Year 2015*, Table 14, http://www.doleta.gov/tradeact/docs/AnnualReport15.pdf.

60. US Department of Labor, Unemployment Insurance Data: Avg. Weekly Benefit in Regular Program, 12 Months Ending 12/31/2016, $344.43, https://ows.doleta.gov/unemploy/DataDashboard.asp.Retrieved Jan. 15, 2017.

61. US Departments of Labor, Commerce, Education, and Health and Human Services (2014, July 22) *What Works in Job Training: A Synthesis of the Evidence*, p. 7-10, https://www.dol.gov/asp/evaluation/jdt/jdt.pdf; Executive Office of the President (2014, July) *Ready to Work: Job-Driven Training and American Opportunity*, p. 7-8, https://obamawhitehouse.archives.gov/sites/default/files/docs/skills_report.pdf

62. US Department of Labor, *Trade Adjustment Assistance for Workers Program: Fiscal Year 2015*, Table 11, http://www.doleta.gov/tradeact/docs/AnnualReport15.pdf

63. US Bureau of Labor Statistics news release, 2019, February 1, https://www.bls.gov/news.release/empsit.nr0.htm Retrieved Feb. 10, 2019.

64. US Congressional Research Service (2014, December 8), *The Cost of Iraq, Afghanistan, and Other Global War on Terror Operations Since 9/11*, Figure 3, https://fas.org/sgp/crs/natsec/RL33110.pdf

65. Congressional Budget Office (2013, February), *Growth in Means-Tested Programs and Tax Credits for Low-Income Households*, p. 32-34 https://www.cbo.gov/publication/43934

66. Levanon, G. and Erumban, A., (2016, April 19). *Help Wanted: What Looming Labor Shortages Mean for Your Business*. Retrieved from The Conference Board. https://www.conference-board.org/press/pressdetail.cfm?pressid=6721

67. Carrick and McNelly. p. 2-5

68. Hochschild, Arlie Russell, *Strangers In Their Own Land: Anger and Mourning on the American Right*, The New Press, New York, 2016

69. Krosch A. and Amodio D., Economic scarcity alters the perception of race, *Proceedings of the National Academy of Sciences*, 2014, vol. 111 no. 25, 9079-9084, cited in: Rhodan M. (2014 June 9), Study: Hard Times Can Make People More Racist, *Time*, www.time.com/2850595/race-economy.

70. Information on Simpson-Bowles Commission from: National Commission on Fiscal Responsibility and Reform, *Wikipedia.org*, https://en.wikipedia.org/wiki/National_Commission_on_Fiscal_Responsibility_and_Reform. Retrieved July 3, 2015.

Additional Reading

(By year of publication)

Kennedy, Paul, *The Rise and Fall of the Great Powers: Economic Change and Military Conflict from 1500 to 2000*, Vintage Books, 1987

Murphy, Cullen, *Are We Rome?: The Fall of an Empire and The Fate of America*, Current Affairs, 2007

Alexander, Jeffrey, *The Performance of Politics: Obama's Victory and the Democratic Struggle for Power*, Oxford University, 2010

Bacevich, Andrew, *The Limits of Power: The End of American Exceptionalism*, Metropolitan Books, 2010

Callahan, David, *Fortunes of Change: The Rise of the Liberal Rich and the Remaking of America*, Wiley, 2010

Codevilla, Angelo, *The Ruling Class: How They Corrupted America, and What We Can Do About It*, American Spectator / Beaufort, 2010

Hacker, Jacob and Pierson, Paul, *Winner-Take-All Politics: How Washington Made the Rich Richer—and Turned Its Back on the Middle Class*, Simon & Schuster, 2010

Hodge, Roger, *The Mendacity of Hope: Barack Obama and the Betrayal of American Liberalism*, Harper/HarperCollins, 2010

Huffington, Arianna, *Third World America: How Our Politicians Are Abandoning the Middle Class and Betraying the American Dream*, Crown, 2010

Rasmussen, Scott, and Schoen, Doug, *Mad As Hell: How the Tea Party Movement is Fundamentally Remaking Our Two Party System*, Harper/HarperCollins, 2010

Cowen, Tyler, *The Great Stagnation: How America Ate All the Low Hanging Fruit of Modern History, Got Sick, and Will (Eventually) Feel Better*, Dutton, 2011

Crier, Catherine, *Patriot Acts: What Americans Must Do to Save the Republic*, Simon & Schuster, 2011

Abramsky, Sasha, *The American Way of Poverty: How the Other Half Still Lives*, Nation Press, 2013

Kissinger, Henry, *World Order*, Penguin Press, 2014

Piketty, Thomas, *Capital in the Twenty-First Century*, Belknap Press, 2014

Tirado, Linda, *Hand to Mouth: Living in Bootstrap America*, G.P. Putnam's Sons, 2014

Amar, Akhil Reed, *America's Unwritten Constitution: The Precedents and Principles We Live By*, Basic Books, 2015

Baradaran, Mehrsa, *How the Other Half Banks: Exclusion, Exploitation, and the Threat to Democracy*, Harvard University Press, 2015

Kay, John, *Other People's Money: The Real Business of Finance*, Public Affairs, 2015

Mayer, Jane, *Dark Money: The Hidden History of the Billionaires Behind the Rise of the Radical Right*, Doubleday, 2015

Putnam, Robert, *Our Kids: The American Dream in Crisis*, Simon & Schuster, 2015

Buckley, FH, *The Way Back: Restoring the Promise of America*, Encounter Books, 2016

Anderson, Carol, *White Rage: The Unspoken Truth of our Racial Divide*, Bloomsbury, 2016

Cole, David, *Engines of Liberty: The Power of Citizen Activists to Make Constitutional Law*, Basic Books, 2016

Das, Satyajit, *The Age of Stagnation: Why Perpetual Growth Is Unattainable and the Global Economy Is in Peril*, Prometheus Books, 2016

Desmond, Matthew, *Evicted: Poverty and Profit in the American City*, Crown Publishers, 2016

Fields, Michelle, *Barons of the Beltway: Inside the Princely World of Our Washington Elite—and How to Overthrow Them*, Crown Forum, 2016

Frank, Thomas, *Listen, Liberal: Or, What Ever Happened to the Party of the People?*, Metropolitan Books / Henry Holt & Company, 2016

Fraser, Steve, *The Limousine Liberal: How an Incendiary Image United the Right and Fractured America*, Basic Books, 2016

Friedman, Thomas, *Thank You for Being Late: An Optimist's Guide to Thriving in the Age of Accelerations*, Farrar, Straus & Giroux, 2016

Gordon, Robert, *The Rise and Fall of American Growth: The US Standard of Living Since the Civil War*, Princeton University Press, 2016

Hacker, Jacob, and Pierson, Paul, *American Amnesia: How the War on Government Led Us to Forget What Made America Prosper*, Simon & Schuster, 2016

Isenberg, Nancy, *White Trash: The 400-Year Untold History of Class in America*, Illustrated, 2016

Jaffe, Sarah, *Necessary Trouble: Americans in Revolt*, Nation Books, 2016

Jones, Robert, *The End of White Christian America*, Simon & Schuster, 2016

Levin, Yuval, *The Fractured Republic: Renewing America's Social Contract in the Age of Individualism*, Basic Books, 2016

Morrissey, Ed, *Going Red: The Two Million Voters Who Will Elect the Next President—And How Conservatives Can Win Them*, Crown Forum, 2016

McChesney, Robert, and Nichols, John, *People Get Ready: The Fight Against a Jobless Economy and a Citizenless Democracy*, Nation Books, 2016

Nesbit, Jeff, *Poison Tea: How Big Oil and Big Tobacco Invented the Tea Party and Captured the GOP*, Thomas Dunne/St. Martin's, 2016

Roth, Zachary, *The Great Suppression: Voting Rights, Corporate Cash, and the Conservative Assault on Democracy*, Crown, 2016

Smith, Steven, *Modernity and Its Discontents: Making and Unmaking the Bourgeois From Machiavelli to Bellow*, Yale University Press, 2016

Stern, Andy, with Kravitz, Lee, *Raising the Floor: How a Universal Basic Income Can Renew Our Economy and Rebuild the American Dream*, Public Affairs, 2016

Trillin, Calvin, *Jackson, 1964: And Other Dispatches From Fifty Years of Reporting on Race in America*, Random House, 2016

Bruder, Jessica, *Nomadland: Surviving America in the Twenty-First Century*, W.W. Norton & Company, 2017

Currid-Halkett, Elizabeth, *The Sum of Small Things: A Theory of the Aspirational Class,* Princeton University Press, 2017

Goodhart, David, *The Road to Somewhere: The Populist Revolt and the Future of Politics*, Hurst, 2017

Grayling, A. C., *Democracy and Its Crisis*, Oneworld, 2017

Haskel, Jonathan, and Westlake, Stian, *Capitalism without Capital: The Rise of the Intangible Economy*, Princeton University Press, 2017

MacLean, Nancy, *Democracy in Chains: The Deep History of the Radical Right's Stealth Plan for America*, Viking, 2017

Reeves Richard, *Dream Hoarders: How the American Middle Class is Leaving Everyone Else in the Dust, Why That Is a Problem, and What to Do About It*, Brookings Institution Press, 2017

Sunstein, Cass, *#Republic: Divided Democracy in the Age of Social Media*, Princeton University Press, 2017

Brettschneider, Corey, *The Oath and the Office: A Guide to the Constitution for Future Presidents*, W.W. Norton & Company, 2018

Giridharadas, Anand, *Winners Take All: The Elite Charade of Changing The World*, Knopf, 2018

Goodwin, Doris Kearns, *Leadership: In Turbulent Times*, Simon & Schuster, 2018

Hedges, Chris, *America: The Farewell Tour*, Simon & Schuster, 2018

Kaufman, Dan, *The Fall of Wisconsin: The Conservative Conquest of a Progressive Bastion and the Future of American Politics*, W.W. Norton & Company, 2018

Lepore, Jill, *These Truths: A History of the United States*, W.W. Norton & Company, 2018

Lessig, Lawrence, *America, Compromised*, The University of Chicago Press, 2018

Lichtman, Allan, *The Embattled Vote in America: From the Founding to the Present*, Harvard University Press, 2018

Pawel, Miriam, *The Browns of California: The Family Dynasty That Transformed a State and Shaped a Nation*, Bloomsbury, 2018

Pinker, Steven, *Enlightenment Now: The Case For Reason, Science, Humanism, and Progress*, Viking, 2018

Posner, Eric, and Weyl, E. Glen, *Radical Markets: Uprooting Capitalism and Democracy for a Just Society*, Princeton University Press, 2018

Smarsh, Sarah, *Heartland: A Memoir of Working Hard and Being Broke in the Richest Country on Earth*, Scribner, 2018

Stanley, Jason, *How Fascism Works: The Politics of Us and Them*, Random House, 2018

Tooze, Adam, *Crashed: How a Decade of Financial Crises Changed the World*, Viking, 2018

Watts, Edward, *Mortal Republic: How Rome Fell into Tyranny*, Basic Books, 2018

Winkler, Adam, *We the Corporations: How American Businesses Won Their Civil Rights*, Liveright, 2018

Acknowledgements

First among those I must thank are Francis Fukuyama, Thomas Mann, and Norman Ornstein. Their clear-eyed analyses of the world as it is, and their tireless advocacy for democratic decency have been an inspiration to me throughout this writing project. My thanks also to my editor, Web Stone, and to former Congressman and US Army Ranger Hall of Fame member Jim Marshall. Their insights and perspectives were always professional and measured, and extremely valuable for the ultimate scope and flow of the book. And finally to my wife Abby and to our children, whose patience, good humor, and love make it all worth the effort.

About The Author

S. J. Reynolds is Senior Associate Director of Corporate Engagement at Princeton University, and founder of the reform group *Principled Power*. He has over twenty-five years of experience in business, the military, and higher education. He began his career as an armor officer in the US Army, then managed technology development and business development for medical and biotechnology companies before joining the staff at Princeton. He continues to serve in the National Guard, with tours in Bosnia and Iraq. Reynolds holds degrees in American history and in management and lives in New Jersey with his family.

Made in the USA
Middletown, DE
22 January 2021